THE

TWELVE STEPS

FOR

SMARTPHONE

ADDICTION

JAMES SUGEL

For more information contact: author@jamessugel.com

First paperback edition March 2019

ISBN 978-1-7329551-0-3 (paperback)
ISBN 978-1-7329551-0-1 (ebook)

jamessugel.com

In memory of my mother,
Elizabeth Claire Sugel

CONTENTS

PREFACE

The rise of computing technology has occurred at an astonishingly rapid pace, and continues to evolve in dramatic fashion. Partially because of this swift rate of change, society has found itself unprepared for certain hidden functions of technological progress. One of these unforeseen consequences is smartphone addiction.

As a result of my computer science degree, I have served in various capacities in information technology over the years, starting in 1987. Working with multiple programming languages and in a diverse array of industries as a software engineer and consultant provided me with practical experience in various technologies.

Thus, I have observed the meteoric advances in computing technology from a first-hand perspective over the last 30 years. Most recently, for the past several years, I've focused on website design and associated technology, search engine optimization, social media strategy, and general digital marketing.

I have always had a necessarily close relationship with technology because of the nature of my career — in retrospect, even an addictive one. However, the introduction of the smartphone changed everything for me and many others.

This device quickly and stealthily came to dominate my life and eventually seemed virtually impossible to live without. But smartphone addiction then was a new and mostly unrecognized phenomenon, with few if any available solutions. However, my lifelong propensity towards addiction and addictive behaviors had provided me with a long history of exposure to a variety of addiction treatments, including involvement in multiple twelve-step programs.

Perhaps because of this combination of twelve-step program experience and constant association with technology, I became acutely aware of the addictive nature of smartphone devices early on. I was thus able to apply twelve-step principles from other programs to the smartphone use in my own life, even though I had not yet formally adapted the twelve steps for smartphone addiction.

Smartphones and the internet didn't exist when I was growing up, but my challenges with other addictions began at a young age.

I got drunk for the first time at an eighth-grade dance. I liked it and acted the fool. This normally shy and quiet boy chased girls at the dance, and lay in the street, laughing uncontrollably, in front of angry drivers on the way home.

Also at thirteen years of age, I overdosed and nearly died after experimenting with a large dosage of barbiturates. I smoked marijuana and took LSD as well for the first time at thirteen. While an intelligent kid, I always felt different and isolated, even around the people who loved me.

Upon entering high school my addiction continued to progress.

My brother Tony, two years older than I, was active in the drug scene and a really hip dude. I tried my best to emulate him and the cool crowd with whom he ran. As a result of my addiction, I eventually found myself in the adolescent psychiatric unit of Rush Medical Center in Chicago at the age of sixteen. It was in that unit that I first became exposed to a twelve-step program. I still have vivid memories of the twelve-step meetings being held in the day room on the eleventh floor, with expansive views of the city lights far below. What immediately caught my attention with the twelve-step program is that some of the counselors and therapists were in the program, as well.

Perhaps too young to stay clean at that time, I got worse and eventually was presented with a dramatic choice at eighteen years old — a long-term drug rehab program or prison. Choosing the rehab program, I was able to stay clean and sober for several years. This intense program, based on a therapeutic community model, featured a diverse array of addiction treatment methodologies, including twelve-step meetings.

Upon attending university I soon discovered I had a talent for coding. I was able to control my other addictions at least partially by fixating on technical projects, and finished college strongly, obtaining a Bachelor of Science, Cum Laude in Computer Science with a second major in Psychology.

Unfortunately, I eventually began to abuse alcohol and other substances, and while I was very bright and did well in software jobs, I got into more and more trouble at work.

After struggling for several years I hit a bottom and entered a twelve-step fellowship. In this program, I worked all twelve steps to the best of my ability and stayed clean and sober for over eight years. During this time, I worked as a software developer and consultant and was very successful. Living the twelve steps as a way of life and attending twelve-step meetings formed the basis of my recovery and success in life for more than eight years.

Near the end of that period, I had realized one of my dreams — moving to Southern California. As a consequence of certain software experience and IBM Professional Certifications I held, I was hired by a software consultancy that was forming a Southern California office. They paid all the expenses for the move. I eventually purchased a nice duplex near the beach in Venice, California.

Externally, my life appeared picture perfect. I lived in my dream location, had a beautiful girlfriend, and a shiny Porsche sat in the driveway. However, my reliance on the twelve steps had faded. As we will see in our analysis of the twelve steps, continuous effort is required to maintain recovery from addiction. Without this spiritual maintenance old addictive thinking and behavior patterns return. The addictive substance or behavior again appears to be a reasonable and effective solution, regardless of the severity of previous consequences caused by the addiction. This condition is often described in twelve-step programs as being "restless, irritable, and discontented." So although I appeared to be very successful, that description fit me perfectly at this time.

I reasoned that I could drink like a gentleman, and in fact deserved this reward due to my success in life. Further use of perverse logic brought me to the conclusion that drugs — specifically my favorite cocaine — had always been the real problem. So if I promised myself to not use cocaine I could drink alcohol without serious consequences. Thus, in June of 2001 I drank again.

Within a week I was drinking too much. I soon discovered that crack cocaine was readily available in Venice. I also discovered that I liked it. My drinking and cocaine use quickly spiraled out of control. I spent all available funds within a few months. Cocaine, expensive liquor, and women were all addictions. Work seemed unimportant and the house went into foreclosure. I sold the property the day before the foreclosure auction, took all the equity proceeds, and moved into a seedy motel on Century Boulevard in Inglewood.

The money was soon gone and on the morning of April 7, 2003 — less than two years after taking that first drink — I was sleeping in a broken down pickup truck parked in a driveway, literally one step from the curb, which was the next destination. The property, close to Century Boulevard in Inglewood California, was just below the flight path into LAX, the Los Angeles International Airport. Three separate groups of addicts lived on the property so there was always plenty of activity — and a veritable cornucopia of drugs and alcohol. But the argumentative addicts, barking dogs, and roaring 747 engines could no longer drown out the reality of my situation. Nor could any amount of alcohol or drugs.

Everything worthwhile in life was gone, and I was alone.

A spiritual epiphany occurred that morning — I knew I had lost my battle with addiction, and that I could never recover on my own.

I entered a drug and alcohol rehab program in Santa Monica, California that day, and have stayed clean and sober ever since.

During this current period of recovery from drug and alcohol addiction, I have established and maintained my sobriety by taking the twelve steps, attending twelve-step meetings regularly, and applying the spiritual principles of the twelve-steps in my life. As mentioned above, my long history of involvement in twelve-step programs allowed me to recognize my addictive tendencies and I was able to apply those same twelve-step principles to my use of technology and eventually to smartphones.

So, over the last few years, as the phenomenon of smartphone addiction became more widely publicized, I often asked myself a question — "Why have the twelve steps not yet been applied to smartphone addiction?"

The answer was always "Someone must be working on it", or "It will happen soon."

Yet it gnawed at me, because each time I went to a tech seminar, or read an article, or saw a news story on smartphone addiction, it seemed clear that the twelve steps were an obvious solution. The twelve steps arguably have been the most successful therapeutic method for treating addictions in human history.

It appeared that perhaps the best potential solution to the serious and growing problem of smartphone addiction was staring us in the face. The twelve steps have provided an effective solution for multiple addictions and a joyous way of life for me, and I believe they can work in your life as well.

Therefore, here is my attempt at applying the twelve steps to smartphone addiction. A high degree of technical education and experience, combined with my battles with addiction and years of recovery in twelve-step programs hopefully provide me with the balance of technical and spiritual background required to produce this work.

I hope that these twelve steps provide individuals with the means to overcome their struggle with this new and powerful addiction.

INTRODUCTION

Addiction can be defined as a craving for a substance or behavior that produces short-term pleasure, over which the user displays an inability to control or stop even in the face of long-term negative consequences.

A smartphone is actually a powerful general-purpose computer that includes cellular phone technology, internet functionality, a user interface, and the ability to install application programs, or apps.

Smartphones have created one of the greatest technological revolutions in human history. They have allowed for an unparalleled access to information and entertainment for users. However, this also entails an unparalleled ability to manipulate the behavior of smartphone users by the businesses that create and control the technology.

One might further conceive of a smartphone as a device that utilizes a synergistic combination of computing and communications technology to allow an individual to connect with other users and access information systems. This connectivity also allows the businesses that create and control the smartphone technology to access data about the individual users and their interactions.

Technology can be broadly defined as the application of

scientific knowledge for practical purposes. In our case, more specifically, technology is the harnessing of information and its use in electronic devices by means of applied sciences.

Smartphone technology and computing technology in general can be divided at the highest level of abstraction into hardware and software. The hardware consists of the physical device and its components, and the software consists of the application programs and the information these programs process.

To conceptualize more broadly, we will want to realize that a smartphone is essentially useless without certain networks. These include cellular communications networks and the internet. Networks are systems that allow for connections between computing devices. These networks also consist of hardware and software like a smartphone but on a much larger scale. Networks are essential for the individual devices to function.

For examining smartphone addiction, we will not attempt to distinguish too much between information and the smartphone device that enables the use of that information. That is, we will not distinguish too much between the software and the hardware. Or between the individual device and the interconnected network to which it belongs.

In other words, is a person addicted to the smartphone or the data? Is it the screen on the device or the app being used? We will assume it is some combination of multiple elements, in that they form a synergistic whole. The device is required for the conveyance of information and is essentially useless without, while the information without the device exists in some form that is unusable in practice, and thus useless without the device. We will also realize that the various network components, both hardware and software, are part of this synergistic system, and thus are elements of a complex system of smartphone technology that creates the addiction.

Another reason for perceiving the device, the essential networks, and the information they process as a unified whole is because technology is progressing so rapidly that our conception of what a smartphone is may change relatively quickly. The twelve steps as conveyed in this work are an attempt to focus on the effects smartphone technology has on the user, thus hopefully remaining independent to some extent of any specific smartphone technology.

The real issue is the effect the use of smartphone technology has on the user, and whether this effect is addictive. As with other addictions, it is probably true that some are more susceptible to becoming addicted than others.

Smartphone addiction is different in certain respects from drug and alcohol addictions; however, there are also many similarities. In fact, one postulate of this work is that smartphone addiction may have potentially more serious consequences than many realize. Later, as we discuss the steps, some similarities and distinctions between other addictions and smartphone addiction will perhaps become clearer.

Based on the most reasonable definitions of addiction, many will agree that smartphone addiction is a real phenomenon. Some will believe outright that they are in fact addicted to their smartphone. In addition, many others will think that someone they know is a smartphone addict. Others will have a suspicion that something is wrong in their relationship to smartphone technology and how it is affecting their lives.

The nature of addiction in general, perspectives on addictions to other substances and behaviors, and a specific focus on the nature of smartphone addiction will be interwoven into our exploration of the twelve steps as it progresses organically.

Nevertheless, the primary purpose of this work is not to define or explain addiction in general, or even smartphone addiction in particular, to any great degree; there is no shortage of works that expand in great depth on these topics. One can easily find many excellent works that focus on the problem of an addiction to smartphones — or any other addiction — and which also provide many concrete examples.

We thus begin with an assumption that society has accepted the reality of smartphone addiction and the fact that it is a troubling and potentially dangerous contemporary phenomenon, even though there may not yet be a generally accepted clinical definition. It follows then that if smartphone addiction is real that the pursuit of possible treatment approaches for this affliction is an important issue in contemporary society.

The primary purpose of this work is to provide a workable solution to the challenge of smartphone addiction. The solution provided is based on the rich and successful concepts of twelve-step programs, first set forth in the book Alcoholics Anonymous, which was initially published in 1939.

While the twelve-step program introduced here is targeted towards smartphone addiction, the concepts are derived from AA as well as other twelve-step programs. As a result, we will use references to some of these programs throughout.

The twelve steps are a program of recovery first published in

1939 in the book Alcoholics Anonymous. They have since been successfully applied to various addictions, through twelve-step programs like Narcotics Anonymous, Gamblers Anonymous, Sex Addicts Anonymous, and many others.

The twelve steps for Smartphone Addiction are adapted with permission from Alcoholics Anonymous and are printed below. The twelve steps of Alcoholics Anonymous are reprinted with permission below as well.

You will note that the twelve steps for Smartphone Addiction are very similar to the original twelve steps of Alcoholics Anonymous and differ for the most part only in the nature of the addiction. The other adaptations of the twelve steps mentioned above are typically very similar to the original twelve steps of Alcoholics Anonymous, as well.

This is because the twelve steps are and have been so spectacularly successful in treating alcoholism and other addictions. One could argue that the twelve steps are the most effective treatment available for alcoholism and other addictions. Now we apply these to the potentially serious societal problems of smartphone addiction.

Each of the twelve steps will be covered in detail further along as they specifically relate to smartphone addiction, but for now, this generic summary of the twelve steps is offered.

Step One suggests the person with the addiction admits they are an addict. In Step Two the addict finds a higher power, and in Step Three turns to that power for help with the addiction.

In Step Four a personal inventory is created, which is disclosed to another in Step Five.

Steps Six and Seven involve analyzing defects of character and turning to the higher power for help with their removal.

In Step Eight a list of those harmed is produced, and in Step Nine amends are made to those on the list.

Steps Ten and Eleven are ongoing maintenance steps, where the addict takes inventory and communicates with their higher power on a daily basis.

Step Twelve suggests that the afflicted individual, now having had a spiritual awakening by working the preceding steps, lives the principles of those steps in his or her daily life, and tries to help others with the same addiction.

Smartphone addiction is a real phenomenon, that because of its recency is only now being fully recognized. The twelve steps have provided an effective solution for many addictions, especially after having been adapted to address those addictions.

Now we apply the twelve steps specifically to smartphone addiction, in the belief that they will prove as successful for this new addiction as they have for so many others.

THE TWELVE STEPS FOR SMARTPHONE ADDICTION

Step One: We admitted we were powerless over our smartphone addiction — that our lives had become unmanageable.

Step Two: Came to believe that a power greater than ourselves could restore us to sanity, particularly in relation to our smartphone use.

Step Three: Made a decision to turn our will and our lives over to the care of our Higher Power, as we understood Him or Her.

Step Four: Made a searching and fearless moral inventory of ourselves, focusing especially on our use of smartphones.

Step Five: Admitted to our Higher Power, to ourselves, and to another person the exact nature of our wrongs.

Step Six: Were entirely ready to have our Higher Power remove our defects of character.

Step Seven: Humbly asked our Higher Power to remove these shortcomings.

Step Eight: Made a list of all persons we had harmed, principally in connection with our smartphone use, and became willing to make amends to them all.

Step Nine: Made direct amends to such people wherever possible, except when to do so would injure them or others.

Step Ten: Continued to take personal inventory, with a special emphasis on our use of smartphones, and when we were wrong promptly admitted it.

Step Eleven: Sought through prayer and meditation to improve our conscious contact with our Higher Power, praying only for knowledge of His or Her will for us and the power to carry that out.

Step Twelve: Having had a spiritual awakening as the result of these steps, we tried to carry this message to other smartphone addicts and to practice these principles in all our affairs.

The twelve steps of Alcoholics Anonymous have been reprinted and adapted with the permission of Alcoholics Anonymous World Services, Inc. ("A.A.W.S."). Permission to reprint and adapt the twelve steps does not mean that Alcoholics Anonymous is affiliated with this program. AA is a program of recovery from alcoholism only — use of AA's Steps or an adapted version in connection with programs and activities which are patterned after AA, but which address other problems, or use in any other non-AA context, does not imply otherwise.

THE TWELVE STEPS OF ALCOHOLICS ANONYMOUS

Step One: We admitted we were powerless over alcohol — that our lives had become unmanageable.

Step Two: Came to believe that a power greater than ourselves could restore us to sanity.

Step Three: Made a decision to turn our will and our lives over to the care of our Higher Power as we understood Him or Her.

Step Four: Made a searching and fearless moral inventory of ourselves.

Step Five: Admitted to our Higher Power, to ourselves, and to another person the exact nature of our wrongs.

Step Six: Were entirely ready to have our Higher Power remove our defects of character.

Step Seven: Humbly asked our Higher Power to remove these shortcomings.

Step Eight: Made a list of all persons we had harmed, and became willing to make amends to them all.

Step Nine: Made direct amends to such people wherever possible, except when to do so would injure them or others.

Step Ten: Continued to take personal inventory and when we were wrong promptly admitted it.

Step Eleven: Sought through prayer and meditation to improve our conscious contact with our Higher Power, praying only for knowledge of His will for us and the power to carry that out.

Step Twelve: Having had a spiritual awakening as the result of these steps, we tried to carry this message to other alcoholics, and to practice these principles in all our affairs.

The twelve steps of Alcoholics Anonymous have been reprinted and adapted with the permission of Alcoholics Anonymous World Services, Inc. ("A.A.W.S."). Permission to reprint and adapt the twelve steps does not mean that Alcoholics Anonymous is affiliated with this program. A.A. is a program of recovery from alcoholism only — use of A.A.'s Steps or an adapted version in connection with programs and activities which are patterned after A.A., but which address other problems, or use in any other non-A.A. context, does not imply otherwise.

STEP ONE

We admitted we were powerless over our
smartphone addiction — that our lives had
become unmanageable.

Most people have trouble admitting they suffer from an addiction. In many cases the addiction continues for years, causing progressively negative consequences in a person's life, before they are willing to admit they have or even may have a problem.

Step One suggests that we are at a point where we are willing to make this admission, or at least entertain the idea that an addictive problem exists. Note that the step is carefully phrased, and asks us to examine our addiction in a possibly new and illuminating light.

There are two distinct yet related concepts that comprise Step One — powerlessness and unmanageability. What does it mean to be "powerless"? What does it mean when something is "unmanageable"? Let's explore these concepts in general and as they are defined in other twelve-step programs first, to get a better conceptual understanding, before applying them to an addiction to smartphone use.

In twelve-step programs, powerlessness means something very specific — the loss of the power of choice over whether to use or not to use the object of the addiction. It will be helpful now to examine how Step One is phrased in some of the traditional twelve-step programs.

In AA, the first step states, "We admitted we were powerless over alcohol — that our lives had become unmanageable."

Step One in the program Narcotics Anonymous specifies, "We admitted we were powerless over our addiction — that our lives had become unmanageable."

The program Sex Addicts Anonymous phrases Step One as, "We admitted we were powerless over addictive sexual behavior — that our lives had become unmanageable."

Overeaters Anonymous utilizes this verbiage for Step One — "We admitted we were powerless over food — that our lives had become unmanageable."

Clearly, in all these cases, the powerlessness is specific to the addictive substance or behavior, and not a general powerlessness over all aspects of one's life. Interestingly, the ultimate reason for this powerlessness is not explicitly defined in Step One in Alcoholics Anonymous or any of the other traditional twelve-step programs.

Meaning that we recognize we are an addict — that we are powerless — based on our reaction to the addictive substance or behavior and the resulting consequences in our lives. The exact cause of the addiction is still unclear. For now at least, rather than search for root causes we recognize and accept the fact that we are an addict. Or at least we are willing to concede that we may have a problem. We will explore this in more detail shortly.

Let us move on to examine the concept of unmanageability, as it is related to powerlessness, and then try to tie the two concepts together to achieve a synergistic understanding of Step One.

Note that as utilized in twelve-step programs we are talking about the unmanageability of "our lives."

What Step One is really telling us is that the powerlessness over the object of our addiction, which we have seen is a very specific phenomenon associated primarily with a particular substance or behavior, has such a profound effect over our choices and actions that it eventually causes a general unmanageability of our lives.

Meaning that the powerlessness that compels a person to engage in the addictive substance or behavior inevitably causes them to make selfish choices that allow them to continue their addiction. This understandably creates problems in multiple areas for the addict. Because the addiction is of paramount importance for them, other aspects of life are necessarily neglected. Unmanageability may appear as deterioration in personal relations, negative consequences at work or school, financial problems, legal issues, challenges in sexual relations, and a host of other potential issues.

Thus, the negative consequences that result from an addictive behavior are the outward manifestation of unmanageability but caused ultimately by the powerlessness over the addiction.

Traditional twelve-step programs believe that the alcoholic or addict has to recognize the nature of the addiction of their own accord before they will move forward with the program of change — that is, taking the twelve steps. Sometimes it is easy to look at someone else and see that they have an addiction that is causing serious problems in their life, but until that person sees this himself or herself and accepts the necessity for help, little can be done for them.

Most people would agree that a real alcoholic or drug addict digs himself or herself into a hole, and at some point, they hit "rock bottom." It has been said that a person hits bottom when they stop digging. The point is that it is not necessary for someone to lose their job, or overdose, or be divorced, or go to prison before they realize they have a problem and accept help.

Therefore, an acceptance of powerlessness and unmanageability over an addictive substance or behavior often involves a realization of the *potential* consequences of the addiction, based on the current circumstances and the fact that addiction is a progressive illness — it always gets worse over time.

It is often easier to see the truth of an addiction in the case of alcohol or drugs because the negative consequences become so severe over time they become hard to deny.

Nevertheless, where smartphone technology is concerned, how does a person determine whether he or she is powerless? Moreover, whether or not his or her life is truly unmanageable, at least as it relates to the smartphone technology in question?

Again, we can look at other twelve-step programs for guidance. As we will see, most such programs have a list of questions that the individual can answer, and if they are answered honestly, may help them to decide whether they have a problem that requires help. There is another common expression in AA, that, "If you find yourself asking if you are an alcoholic or not, you probably are because non-alcoholics don't ask that question." This is somewhat tongue in cheek, but there is a lot of truth to the statement as well.

We have seen that the way the powerlessness manifests itself in a person's life is through the resultant unmanageability. Can a person really be "powerless" over the use of a smartphone? In addition, can the use of a smartphone really make a person's life "unmanageable"?

Let us take a case where the answer is easier to determine — gaming. In extreme cases, the person loses touch with reality, possibly locking them self in a room, and not eating. In this case it is clear that an addiction is at work and that the powerlessness over the gaming — the use of gaming technology — has created unmanageability in the individual's life.

However, in most cases, a smartphone addiction is not as apparent. The inability to not use the smartphone — the powerlessness — and the negative consequences caused by this — the unmanageability — are often more subtle and difficult to perceive. After all, smartphone technology has become such a ubiquitous and essential part of modern life, so thoroughly woven into the fabric of our era, that it may seem impossible to differentiate addictive behavior from legitimate necessity.

Yet most people who are asking whether they have an addiction to smartphones or not will realize that smartphone technology actually dominates their life in many ways. Many of us are truly addicted to our smartphones.

So how does one determine whether or not they are an addict? Most twelve-step adherents and addiction specialists believe that until the addicted person admits they have the problem very little can be done for them. So addiction may be thought of as a disease or condition that requires a self-diagnosis, at least for the person to begin to recover.

One common method used by many traditional twelve-step programs is some variations of the 20 Questions, first conceived by Dr. Robert Seligman of Johns Hopkins University in the 1930's. The idea was that if the person answered one question "yes", this was a warning that they may be an alcoholic. If they answered two in the affirmative, there was a good chance they were an alcoholic; moreover, if they answered three or more positively, they were categorized as an alcoholic.

A pamphlet actually published by Alcoholics Anonymous in 1956 titled, *Is AA for You? Twelve Questions Only You Can Answer* asked twelve questions about the potential alcoholic. This pamphlet states that if you answer four or more of these in the affirmative then you are probably in trouble with alcohol.

A similar set of questions exists for most traditional twelve-step programs. Narcotics Anonymous has a twenty-five questions method. Gamblers Anonymous uses a twenty questions approach. Another successful twelve-step program, Overeaters Anonymous, uses a fifteen questions method. Readers are encouraged to research these specific documents and the rich body of literature these traditional twelve-step programs have to offer.

The twenty questions listed below are meant to perform a similar function for our purpose, that of determining whether or not a person has a problem with smartphone addiction. They borrow liberally from all the traditions mentioned above and thus are not new or creative to any great degree.

There also is no research associated with the selection of the questions, so they are decidedly unscientific. They are but an attempt to create a set of questions that reasonably search for a way that a person might begin to see if they have a problem with addiction to smartphone technology.

The 20 Questions — Are You A Smartphone Addict?

1) Does the use of your smartphone interfere with your sleeping?

2) Has your smartphone usage interfered with or affected your personal relationships?

3) Do you ever feel remorse about the way you use your smartphone?

4) Does your use of a smartphone boost or lower your self-esteem?

5) Does your use of a smartphone cause financial problems (e.g., gambling, shopping, or purchasing of hardware or software products)?

6) Does your smartphone use negatively affect your work performance?

7) Do positive or negative reinforcements from your smartphone cause you to continue to use it when you know you should stop?

8) Do you lose time from school because of your use of a smartphone?

9) Has your smartphone use affected your reputation among your family, friends, school, or business?

10) Do you try to schedule or control the use of your smartphone but find that you really cannot?

11) Does good fortune drive you to use your smartphone?

12) Does misfortune compel you to use your smartphone?

13) Do you feel an obsessive urge to use your smartphone to escape feelings of boredom or loneliness?

14) Do you crave your smartphone after a short time without it?

15) Have you substituted one smartphone app for another, thinking for example that Facebook is the problem and switching to Instagram?

16) Do you feel an urge to use your smartphone as soon as you awaken?

17) Have you ever stolen to enable your continued smartphone use?

18) Have you lied to or manipulated others to further your use of a smartphone?

19) Do you feel it would be almost impossible to live without the uncontrolled use of your smartphone?

20) Do you use a smartphone to enhance or replace normal sexual

relationships, or has your use of a smartphone affected your sex life in some other way?

There is no set number of "yes" answers that can clearly tell a person whether they are a smartphone addict. However, I think if a person answers these questions honestly, they will often know the answer for themselves.

These twenty questions will be revisited later when we discuss Step Four, the personal inventory step, as they will be helpful at that point in our journey of recovery.

One of the defining characteristics of alcoholism, as set forth in the book Alcoholics Anonymous, is "the phenomenon of craving." As described in our initial definition of addiction and many other definitions, this craving is also inherent in all addictions. The perspective of the current work is that this phenomenon of craving — the distinguishing characteristic of all addictions — is just as real for the smartphone addict as it is for the heroin addict or alcoholic.

We crave the use of smartphone technology and its constant and effective system of sensory rewards in a strikingly similar way to any other addict. Additionally, just like any other addict who realizes they are powerless and their life is unmanageable, smartphone addicts must find help in a power greater than themselves, or suffer the debilitating consequences of a chronic and progressive enslavement to smartphone technology.

STEP TWO

Came to believe that a power greater than ourselves could restore us to sanity.

Step Two introduces the concept of a higher power. That is, any power greater than the self that the afflicted addict can turn to for help with the addiction.

One perspective on the steps beyond the first, which comprise any twelve-step program, is that the action of a particular step is contained in the subsequent step. That is, the action suggested by a step is a logical consequence of an acceptance of the principles or the conclusions afforded by the previous step.

So, if one accepts the conclusion drawn in Step One — that of personal powerlessness over a particular substance or behavior — it follows that without the help of some external power the afflicted individual cannot recover from the addicted condition.

In the case of drugs or alcohol, it is often easier to realize the dire consequences of continued addiction. The consensus is that because these are fatal illnesses the person may eventually die from the addiction. Even the addict or alcoholic can often see this as a very real and even likely potential result.

Thus, the well-known sentence often heard in recovery meetings and addiction treatment programs — "The only outcomes for the addict are jails, institutions, and death."

There is a fourth implicit possible outcome, though — that of recovery. Meaning the addict or alcoholic works the steps of the appropriate twelve-step program, starting with recognition of the nature of the disease in Step One and then finding a higher power. Or they may stop using or drinking via some other non-twelve-step method, like reliance on a particular religion or psychotherapy.

As discussed above and in Step One, for a drug addict or alcoholic it is sometimes easier to accept the notion of personal powerlessness over the addiction and thus see the necessity of finding and turning to some external power for help. Because if you do not you are going to die.

This seems a bit severe in the case of smartphone addiction, so we must perhaps adjust our perspective. We come to realize that smartphone technology typically damages our lives in a different yet ultimately progressively negative manner. In addition, although the dangerous and potentially fatal consequences of an addiction to smartphone technology may not be as apparent they do exist, like dying in an auto accident while texting. However, for the most part, the effects of smartphone addiction are much more subtly pernicious.

Thus, although the detrimental consequences are not usually as severe as those of traditional addictions, if we accept the principle of personal powerlessness over our smartphone use we still must find help from some power greater than ourselves if we are to recover from this addiction.

All twelve-step programs have a strong spiritual component. One twelve-step perspective on the use of alcohol and drugs is that the addict distances them self from spirituality by the use of the addictive substance. Once this spiritual hole is filled again by a higher power, the obsession — the phenomenon of craving — for the addictive substance or behavior is lifted.

This means that we must discuss the nature of a higher power, or God if you will.

One of the great insights into addiction recovery delivered to the world through Alcoholics Anonymous is the concept of a truly personal understanding of a higher power. As related by Bill Wilson in many speeches and in the book Alcoholics Anonymous, Ebby Thacher, the man who carried the message of a possible spiritual solution to Bill, said to Bill in their famous meeting over the kitchen table "Why don't you choose your own conception of God?"

This is why all real twelve-step programs are not religious, but spiritual. No particular beliefs or religious practices are required, yet none are banned or discouraged either.

The truly beautiful nature of the spiritual relationship formed and strengthened through a twelve-step program is that of an intensely personal one.

Some people coming into a twelve-step program have a very strong conception of spirituality and a powerful and intimate connection with God or whatever their conception of a higher power may be. They may have strong religious practices and belong to a particular religion. This is fantastic and sometimes makes it easier to accept Step Two and move on to Step Three.

Others may be agnostic, or even atheistic. These people often find a higher power of their own understanding though, if they can be open-minded and willing.

The idea is that a person simply agrees that there is some power greater than they are. This is not too difficult. It has been said that if you do not believe there is a power greater than yourself go stand on the shore at the ocean and try to stop the waves. This may seem somewhat tongue-in-cheek but contains an important starting point for discovering a higher power — the natural world.

The brilliant sun is obviously a greater power than any human is. A lofty mountain towers over us, standing tall for millennia and witnessing the rise and fall of countless civilizations. All humans have within some intuitive conception and ultimate connection with a natural universal power from which we originate and eventually return.

Thus, the terms of twelve-step programs for finding a higher power are very open and forgiving. At some point we wish to grow that conception into something of a personal relationship. But to begin all we need is to admit there is a power greater than ourselves, and come to believe that we can turn to that power for help with our addictive problem.

A further concept inherent in Step Two is that of insanity. In twelve-step programs, an oft-repeated phrase is "Insanity is repeating the same behavior over and over expecting different results."

This is true but is only part of the characteristics of the thinking and behavior that define an addict. Sometimes the addict repeats the same behavior over and over *knowing* what the results will be. Moreover, sometimes they do not think at all and end up indulging in the addictive behavior through what appears to be some type of subconscious or even unconscious process.

Here we are talking about the particular insanity that compels the individual always to return to the addictive substance or behavior, regardless of the consequences.

Therefore, even for alcoholics or addicts the insanity suggested in Step Two is not a generalized or clinical insanity, but some peculiar mental twist specific to the particular addiction that essentially forces the addict to engage in the addiction. An important component of twelve-step programs is the idea that one's own personal willpower is useless as it applies to the addiction, no matter how intelligent or capable they may be in other areas of life.

Again, it is perhaps much easier in many cases for an alcoholic or drug addict to recognize their thinking and behavior as "insanity," than it is for someone with a smartphone addiction, or even some of the other addictions for which a twelve-step methodology exists.

In fact, Gamblers Anonymous(GA), one of the earliest and most successful adaptations of the AA program applied to another addiction, constructs Step Two as "Came to believe that a Power greater than ourselves could restore us to a normal way of thinking and living."

What would "insanity" mean then, as it applies to a smartphone addiction? Just as with other addictions, it means that our human logic and rationality can rarely, if ever, solve the problem. This is humbling because we pride ourselves on our ability to apply logic to a situation and figure it out.

Insanity in the case of smartphone addiction means using the device even when we know that use is harming others or us. It means returning to our devices even when we do not really *need* to use them. It means returning to our devices even when we do not really *want* to use them. It means mindlessly picking up the device and not even knowing we did. Perhaps the most pernicious and inexplicable component of the insanity of addiction, as the book Alcoholics Anonymous says of alcoholism, is "the utter inability to leave it alone, no matter how great the wish."

If you have made conscious, rational, and determined decisions to control your smartphone use yet cannot seem to achieve these goals, is this not a form of insanity? A specific and peculiar form of insanity, very carefully constrained to this particular case?

A subtler manifestation of the insanity of smartphone addiction is the negative effect our selfish and self-centered use of the technology may have on our personal relationships. We will examine this important consequence in more detail later.

So, if we accept that some power greater than ourselves is required to relieve us of the insanity that characterizes our smartphone addiction, we must then resolve to turn to that power and place the problem in the hands of that power. This means that we are suffering from an affliction that can only be arrested through a spiritual experience, which begins with a decision to cooperate fully with our own higher power.

STEP THREE

Made a decision to turn our will and our lives over to the care of our higher power as we understood him or her.

Step Three is the logical action catalyzed by Step Two. If we believe a power greater than ourselves can help us, we now turn to that power and explicitly request help for our addiction.

A key principle associated with Step Three in traditional twelve-step programs is willingness. In this case, to do something about our addiction, based on the conclusions reached in Steps One and Two.

Like all of the twelve steps, the verbiage of Step Three is carefully chosen and pregnant with meaning. Let us now examine the constituent elements of the step individually to arrive at a clear understanding.

Made a decision...

Interestingly, Step Three states that we "made a decision to ...". An understanding of this portion of the step is crucial to our working this step and subsequent steps.

What does it mean to "make a decision?" Why not just say, "Turned our will and lives over to the care of God as we understood him", leaving out the "Made a decision to …" portion? The verbiage of the step is intentional and has an important yet hidden meaning.

A simple parable that has been used in other twelve-step programs to enhance understanding of this phrase follows: "Three frogs are perched on a log at the edge of a pond. One frog decides to jump in the pond. How many frogs are left on the log?"

Many people say "two", reasoning that one frog jumped in the pond. Three minus one is two, of course, so the answer seems obvious.

Yet the correct answer is three frogs remain on the log. Our decision-making frog only *made a decision* to jump — he did not actually jump.

The poignant principle behind this choice of verbiage is action. Meaning that any decision — choice, if you will — is only just that until some physical action is taken based on the decision. We will see the importance of this concept later in our discussion.

To turn our will and our life...

Interestingly, the step says to turn our will *and* our life over to the care of God, as we understood him. This implies that there is some important distinction between the words "will" and "life" for an understanding and implementation of the step.

Will might be simply defined as one's thoughts and desires. One of the key concepts of many twelve-step programs is that of the misuse of the will, by directing it via selfish motives that often are hidden to the individual. After all, a selfish and self-centered person usually does not believe they are selfish and self-centered.

In the book Alcoholics Anonymous a great deal of effort is spent on exploring the concept of selfishness in the explanation of Step Three. It may seem confusing or inappropriate at first glance to associate selfishness with Step Three, but one of the goals of twelve-step programs is to distinguish between our own will and that of our higher power.

However, why are the words "and life" appended to the step? If the misuse or misdirection of our will and the subsequent inability to differentiate the will of our higher power from our own is the key, why include life?

Again, the answer is profound once disclosed. Our life includes many things that are completely external to our will. Events that are outside our locus of control altogether.

The economy, the weather, accidents, disease — all these are examples of events or categories that can affect us dramatically, but over which our will has no bearing. An example is the diagnosis of a terminal illness in a loved one. This had, and has, nothing to do with our will, but definitely affects our life. When a car runs a red light and smashes into us, putting us in a hospital bed for a month, this clearly has a drastic effect on us, but the cause has nothing to do with our will.

Therefore, by phrasing the step as "our will and our life," we turn over to our higher power everything over which we have any control, and also everything over which we have no control as well.

The phrasing of the remainder of the step is one of the primary reasons that twelve-step programs have been so successful for so many people.

When the book Alcoholics Anonymous was being written, Bill

Wilson would send chapters or portions to select members of the program for review. One of the most heated topics of debate was whether to use religious terminology in the text. The extension to God *"as we understood him,"* was compromised language agreed upon after some debate.

Consider the profound difference in adoption of the step, and of twelve-step programs in general, if the more absolute language of, "Made a decision to turn our will and our lives over to the care of God," had been used. The modifier "as we understood him" simplifies and softens the message of the step dramatically.

As mentioned above in the discussion on Step Two, one of the most profound contributions of AA to spirituality in human history is this concept of a personal relationship with and potentially imperfect understanding of a higher power, with no dogmatic belief system required.

So if in Step Two we either confirmed our already held spiritual beliefs, or began to formulate some new personal conception of a spiritual connection, in Step Three we take a true leap of faith by turning our will and lives over to that power.

Again though, it may seem reasonable that such a dramatic decision as this step suggests may be necessary for an alcoholic or a drug addict, whose very life hangs in balance based on the nature of their disease, but is this necessary for an addiction to smartphone technology? In addition, do the same concepts and terminology of Step Three apply? The answer is yes, if we examine carefully what we have discovered on our journey thus far.

How is selfishness the root of our troubles when we are discussing smartphone addiction?

Smartphone technology can form a barrier between ourselves and those around us. It separates us from other people, and from our loved ones. It also serves to separate us from our higher power, or God if you prefer.

This separation is often at a subconscious level, but so is that of an alcoholic or drug addict. The real key to understanding the important implications of this step is again the idea of self-will and selfishness. Our use of smartphones is often selfish. We ignore our loved ones, we disobey traffic laws, and we are rude around others in public. We may even be pulled subtly from our spiritual practice and our connection to a higher power, by the alluring and persistent pull of smartphone technology.

As mentioned previously, the action of a step can be regarded as being contained in the next step. Though our decision in Step Three is of fundamental importance in moving forward with the spiritual solution of the steps, it by itself has little permanent effect. The decision must be followed immediately by a deep and searching look at ourselves, especially in relation to our smartphone use. This is a concerted attempt to uncover the often-hidden characteristics of self that actually drive our selfish behavior.

STEP FOUR

Made a searching and fearless moral inventory of ourselves, focusing especially on our use of smartphones.

Step Four suggests that the addicted individual perform a personal inventory, which is intended to uncover the underlying causes of the addictive behavior. This process involves a thorough look at our thought processes and emotions, our relations with others, and our behaviors relative to smartphone technology. We are especially searching for the deep-seated psychological and emotional defects behind our selfish motives, and an examination of the resulting negative choices and subsequent behaviors that may have harmed other people or ourselves.

Inventory Approaches from Traditional Twelve-Step Programs

In traditional twelve-step programs and ours as well, the fourth step process is referred to as a "moral" inventory.

For instance, in AA, Step Four is phrased, "Made a searching and fearless moral inventory of ourselves."

In Gamblers Anonymous(GA), one of the earliest and most

successful adaptations of the AA program, Step Four is constructed as, "Made a searching and fearless moral and financial inventory of ourselves."

Overeaters Anonymous uses an unmodified version of AA's Step Four, "Made a searching and fearless moral inventory of ourselves", as does Narcotics Anonymous.

Let us consider the use of the term moral in this step, since the word may conjure up an image of being smacked on the hand with a ruler by a school teacher and thus misunderstood in our present context. We can define moral as that which is concerned with principles of right and wrong behavior.

The word principle is crucial here because if one is acting on unethical principles clearly those principles can then be used to justify unethical motives and subsequent unethical behaviors. It seems almost a tautology that a selfish person does not perceive himself or herself as being selfish. Thus, one perspective on selfishness is that we are acting on incorrect or morally wrong principles, but somehow believing that they are correct or morally right, thereby displaying a misunderstanding of what constitutes an ethically correct principle.

How then are we to determine what are the right principles on which to base our motives and behavior?

We may have to step back even further to a more primitive level. More than we like to admit, many of our motives and behaviors are based on instinct rather than on an analysis of principle.

The misuse of instincts can be seen as causing most of our emotional problems. Our instincts for security, sex, power, and belonging can be powerful, subtle — and often unconscious — drivers of our motives and decisions.

In traditional twelve-step programs, it is thought that a solitary, internal examination of ourselves is seldom if ever sufficient to discover the real causes of one's behavior. The same deep-seated, primeval, emotional instincts that control our thinking tend to override our vaunted rationality and justify our actions through some usually hazy logic.

Thus, the emphasis placed on a written inventory. Putting the inventory on paper, assuming that effort and honesty are in effect, produces a tangible result that is difficult to deny or rationalize. The concept of the cathartic effect offered by writing is well known. Therefore, we are really examining our obvious wrong behaviors first since these are easiest to see. We are then in a position to determine the underlying causes after some further analysis.

Traditional twelve-step programs thus perceive the object of the addiction — whether it be drugs, alcohol, sex, or whatever — as a symptom of an underlying problem or set of problems. In our case, it is not liquor or drugs but smartphone technology and our relation to it that is the symptom.

Again, we must reiterate what we are trying to achieve here. We are really attempting to obtain an objective perspective based on our underlying motives, subsequent choices, and consequent actions relative to our use of smartphone technology.

It is particularly important that we focus on the effects our misuse or overuse of our smartphones has in respect to our relations with others. The harms we have perpetrated in our personal relations, and our relationship with a higher power, are at the core of Step Four. Then we may see a bit more clearly why selfishness is at the root of our addictive relationship with our smartphones.

Selfishness can be summed up in a simple two-word sentence — "I want." Often this selfish desire is subconscious, as we have already discussed, and so it is only by objectively examining our behavior and really digging deep into the underlying motives behind our choices that we can see that we essentially misuse technology because it feels good, although we dismiss or rationalize most or all negative consequences.

Beneath this selfishness, we often find that undeserved pride, emotional insecurity, and immaturity are at the core of our problem.

Thus, in the inventory process, we come to realize that it is our underlying "defects of character" that drive us into addiction.

So how does one actually make a searching and fearless moral inventory for smartphone addiction? Let us first examine the development of this concept in traditional twelve-step programs to gain a thorough understanding of the history and intent of the fourth step. We can then construct an inventory method, or methods, based on these traditional approaches that are tailored to smartphone addiction.

An important influence on the two co-founders of Alcoholics Anonymous and the development of AA's twelve steps was the Oxford Group, a Christian organization that was very popular in the 1930s. The founder, American Missionary Frank Buchman, believed that root of all problems were personal fears and selfishness. Furthermore, that the solution to these problems was to surrender one's life to God.

Both Bill Wilson and Dr. Bob Smith, the co-founders of Alcoholics Anonymous, were Oxford Group members and actually met through Oxford Group affiliations.

The Oxford Group program from which Alcoholics Anonymous obtained many of its concepts included a moral inventory process. It was phrased, "We made a moral inventory of our defects or sins." Thus one perspective on a "moral" inventory, albeit a Christian based one, would be to examine our behavior in relation to the seven deadly sins. These, of course, are pride, greed, gluttony, sloth, envy, lust, and anger. In fact, the chapter corresponding to moral inventory in the 1933 text "What Is the Oxford Group?" is titled simply "Sin." It discusses sin in general terms but does not really define an inventory method.

One of the primary precepts of the Oxford Group were the Four Absolutes. These are Absolute Honesty, Absolute Purity, Absolute Unselfishness, and Absolute Love. These were thought to be the keys to right thinking, right living, and correct moral relationship between God and man.

Apocryphal evidence suggests that one way Oxford Group adherents took their inventories was through using these concepts. Oxford Group members reported taking a sheet of paper and folding it so there were four quadrants. They would then write one of the four absolutes in each quadrant and then write below about how they measured up to these absolutes.

Once the twelve-step program was developed and published by Alcoholics Anonymous, there were detailed suggested methods for taking the inventory in the exposition of Step Four. But this was not always true.

One little-known fact about AA is that although the birth date of the program is June 10, 1935, the book Alcoholics Anonymous was not published until 1939. This book is often referred to in

AA and other recovery programs as "The Big Book". It was written, primarily by Bill Wilson, in 1938 and 1939. Bill Wilson while writing the book composed the twelve steps. Even the name of the program, Alcoholics Anonymous, was created while the book was being produced and so did not exist before 1939. Thus, prior to the final form of the steps being produced and codified in book form in 1939, there were several years where different approaches of "working a program" were used by early members of the group that would become AA.

These early members of the program that would become AA first utilized the Oxford Group program. One of the reasons AA moved away from the Oxford Group was the concept of the four Absolutes described above. These were thought to be too strict for an alcoholic to achieve reasonable adherence.

At some point, AA operated with an informal word of mouth six-step program. In this program, Step Two was "Got honest with ourselves." There is evidence that written inventories were a part of this process, although it appears that this process was somewhat ad hoc.

So, it was not until the book Alcoholics Anonymous was published with its twelve steps in 1939 that a definite suggested method of taking an inventory existed.

The process as laid out in the book is divided into an analysis of three areas — resentments, fears, and sex. Resentment comes first for AA, described in the text as "the number one offender." We can consider resentment as the defect, or sin, of anger.

The book then describes the most common method utilized in traditional twelve-step programs, by which the inventory taker creates a set of columns. In the first column, the person, institution, or principle against whom or towards the resentment is directed is listed. In column two the actual event or series of events that caused the resentment are listed. In column three the part of self that is hurt by the causative event is delineated.

The book then reasons that other people are often wrong. In twelve-step programs, a famous line one might hear from a member when discussing their inventory is, "I had to look at that fourth column." This refers to the part in the text that suggests we had to look at where we were at fault in each of the situations, because historically a person only looks at the mistakes of others in a situation, and often not their own. Therefore, in column four the person tries honestly to note where they were at fault in causing the resentment. Then column five lists the primary defect of character causing our fault. We will look into defects of character at greater length later.

The AA text then discusses fear, suggesting we put the fears on paper. We then examine why we have the fear. Although the column example is not explicitly given for fears, the most common way of doing the inventory in AA and other programs uses a similar set of columns for fears as the one for resentments that we have discussed already.

Next, an examination of the individual's sex conduct is suggested. As with fears, the column methodology is usually used in practice although not explicitly spelled out in the AA text.

While the book Alcoholics Anonymous is the foundation of that twelve-step program and all subsequent ones, there is also another important AA text relating to the steps. This is the Twelve

Steps and Twelve Traditions, known informally as the Twelve and Twelve, published in 1952. This book, like the AA Big Book, was written primarily by Bill Wilson, and is a further testament to his spiritual genius.

The Twelve and Twelve was produced with 13 years of practical experience working the steps after the AA Big Book was published in 1939, and expands on the suggestions and ideas of the steps as initially described in the AA Big Book. The Step Four chapter in the Twelve and Twelve is especially notable for its new approaches to taking inventory. Many AA members use both the AA Big Book and the Twelve and Twelve, for in combination they provide a powerful basis for an inventory.

One perspective on the inventory discussed here is to examine our behavior in relation to the seven deadly sins. These, of course, are pride, greed, gluttony, sloth, envy, lust, and anger.

Another innovation of the Twelve and Twelve relative to Step Four is the numerous questions listed. It is suggested that the alcoholic examine his or her life and behaviors using these questions about relationships and financial matters to further expand the inventory.

Another method often used in twelve-step programs in conjunction with the columns and questions is to have the inventory taker write out his or her life story. This helps to obtain a clear perspective on the entirety of one's existence. Important events that may have been the cause of future negative choices may be unearthed in the story. The story also provides a sort of feedback mechanism for the columns and questions, and vice versa.

Most twelve-step programs, because they are all based on AA, use similar approaches for the most part, although they may differ in specifics.

Another simpler approach to performing a moral inventory that is sometimes used in traditional twelve-step programs is to take a sheet of paper and create two columns, one labeled *Assets*, and the other *Liabilities*. Then the intrepid inventory taker lists these as appropriate.

An even simpler approach asks the individual to simply list all his or her secrets and the worst harms they have caused, without a large amount of detail.

Therefore, we see that there are many possible approaches to completing a moral inventory in a twelve-step program. However, note that in all twelve-step programs it is strongly suggested that the inventory be in written form.

Inventory for Smartphone Addiction

How then, shall we propose to perform an inventory for our specific situation, that of a thorough analysis of our motives, choices, and actions as they relate to our smartphone use?

A good beginning is to remember that in Step Three we made a decision to turn our will and our life over to our higher power. Now we can begin to implement that decision by asking our higher power to help us face our negative behaviors and motives and to reveal the defects that have caused us and those around us pain and suffering.

This communication, or prayer, might include a request that we are provided with the courage and insight to be truly searching and fearless in our inventory, so that the information we uncover about ourselves might improve our relationships with our fellow human beings and our higher power.

Our suggested method for taking an inventory for smartphone addiction will follow the most commonly used format in many twelve-step programs as already described briefly, that of creating lists for resentments, fears, and sex conduct. We will then also review the 20 questions for smartphone addiction as part of our inventory process.

As described earlier, there are other methods used for performing a fourth step inventory in traditional twelve-step programs. As experience with the Twelve Steps for Smartphone Addiction grows other methods may be utilized, but for now we will adapt the original twelve-step approach.

Inventory of Resentments

Let us start the actual inventory process with a list of people, principles, or institutions we dislike or even hate. Usually, we have what we think is a solid reason for our negative feelings. Moreover, sometimes it is true that others have mistreated us, although we often discover through this inventory process that we have played our part.

Hence, we list each name in one column, the harm they caused us in the second, and the way this made us feel in the third. Traditional twelve-step programs call this a list of resentments.

Resentment might be defined as the feeling of displeasure or anger at some event, person, statement, or organization regarded by the offended party as causing injury or insult. Note that the first use of the word is in French, but the etymology is the

Latin words "re" meaning "again and again" and "sentir" meaning "to feel". Thus, a resentment really means to *feel* anger about an event repeatedly.

You may wonder, "What does this have to do with the use of my smartphone?" Because while some of the items on our resentment list may be directly related to our smartphone use, others may seem to have nothing at all in common with our addiction.

An example may be in order. Let us say your boss at work has criticized you on occasion for playing around on Facebook during work meetings. You know you do it, but you are upset because you feel you do a good job. You ask yourself, "Why does he keep bothering me?" You believe that a reasonable personal use of your smartphone at work is normal and that it does not affect your productivity in any negative way. In fact, it enhances your productivity by allowing you to release stress. Besides, everybody does it.

The above example is clearly related to the use of a smartphone in an ethically questionable manner. A thorough inventory will disclose many examples like this, and they are at the core of our inventory.

Shall we though, include other grudges that seem to have nothing to do with our smartphone use?

Again, an example is apropos. Your co-worker is a real busybody. She gossips to everyone and you are sometimes the target of the gossip. No one trusts her, but everyone listens.

It is best practice in taking an inventory — because we have agreed at the outset to take a searching and fearless one — to list *all* of our resentments. The reason is that we may find that some of the feelings and defects beneath these seemingly unrelated resentments are really the ones that underlie our sometimes-unhealthy relationship with our smartphones.

So while some may want to list only those grudges specifically related to smartphone use, others who want to dig deeper will list all resentments, and later determine whether they are related or not.

In any event, once we have the three columns for a person, principle or institution, we will then move on to what is often considered the most important part of such an inventory — our part in the matter. This then becomes column four.

We will want to carefully look at each instance and try to determine where we were at fault. Usually, if we truly try to apply an honest and objective perspective on the matter, we will see that we have some part in it.

This is because almost all resentments that we nurse are due to something we did, although we often do not see it. In fact, one might say that holding a resentment often requires some form of self-justification or rationalization.

Having said this, it is also true that there may be cases where we have done nothing wrong. If someone breaks into your car and steals your smartphone with all your information, you probably really did nothing to create the event that caused your resentment.

However, one might argue that the holding of the resentment itself is wrong. Traditional twelve-step programs believe that the anger, whether justified or not, can cause us to turn from our higher power and our fellows, and possibly compel us subconsciously to escape into our addictive behavior. So if one wants to create a thorough inventory, it may be best to list every resentment, whether we think it is related to smartphone use or not.

A fifth column then adds what we perceive as the underlying defect of character that drove our bad motive or behavior. Usually, these are fear, selfishness, immaturity, or pride. When we work Steps Six and Seven we will explore the nature of defects in more detail, so do your best at this point and do not worry about getting too specific or psychoanalytical.

Here is a suggested format for taking such an inventory of resentments for smartphone addiction, with some examples of how inventory entries might be constructed.

Suggested Format for Inventory of Resentments

Whom Do I Have A Resentment For?	The Cause	What Part of Self Is Affected?	What Did I Do? My Part	Defect Causing My Part
My Boss	Criticized me in front of my co-workers for social media use at work	Self-esteem Economic Security	Used social media for personal use on company time	Selfishness Insecurity FOMO
My Girlfriend	She found sex images on my phone	Sexual instinct Insecurity Self esteem	Looked at images of other girls when I'm supposed to be in a committed relationship	Lust FOMO Pride
Jim Seymour	His posts get more engagement than mine	Insecurity Self esteem	Rely on digital signals for my self-esteem	Insecurity Pride

It may be difficult in some cases to find material for columns four and five, but the effort put forth at this point may lead to deep insights into our psyche that make us better people and allow us to understand our relationship with smartphone technology more clearly.

Inventory of Fears

Traditional twelve-step inventories promote a self-analysis of our fears. Moreover, it focuses on how these fears affect our motives and actions. Many of us come to realize that fear or some aspect of it is a major controlling force in our lives. Fear may be disguised by other defects of character, at least in part because most of us do not like to admit we are afraid. Admission of fear can make one feel vulnerable, and a fear may be thus cloaked by some other emotion like anger or sadness.

As with our inventory of resentments, we construct a list of our fears. Column one contains the person, event, or idea that is the object of the fear. The second column then searches for the cause of the fear related to the item in column one. Column three then examines the part of self that is affected by the fear.

Just as with our resentment inventory, the crux of our inventory of fears lies in columns four and five. In column four, we ask where we were at fault. Meaning what action or thought we took or maintained that led to or nurtured the fear. In column five, we again try to list the underlying defect of character that seems to be the root cause of the fear.

Here is a suggested format for taking such an inventory of fears for smartphone addiction, with some examples of how inventory entries might be constructed.

Suggested Format for Inventory of Fears

Who or What Do I Fear?	The Cause	What Part of Self Is Affected?	What Did I Do to Bring on the Fear?	Defect Causing My Part
Losing My Phone	I have lost it before and felt super insecure	Self-esteem Economic Security	Rely too much on my phone	Selfishness Insecurity FOMO
Losing My Job	I've been criticized at work	Insecurity Self esteem	Used phone at work	Insecurity Pride
Generalized FOMO	Always have to know everything that's going on	Insecurity Self esteem	Use the device for information instead of people	Insecurity Pride

Often the root cause of a fear turns out to be selfishness. We fear that we will not get something we want or we fear that we will lose something we already have.

A major fear related to smartphone use is, of course, the infamous "fear of missing out," or FOMO. This drives us constantly to check our devices in order to make sure we do not miss anything important. If everyone else knows about something and we do not we feel left out.

However, how often are these "important" events really important? We will want to ask ourselves what real emotion is at the basis of our FOMO. Is it a desire for belonging? A fear of rejection? In addition, what is behind a fear of rejection? Self-consciousness? Some old emotional wound that we avoid touching?

This is an example of why a shallow surface-level inventory may be insufficient. Usually, if we do have some deep-seated emotional scars they are in that position of our psyche for a reason — they are painful and traumatic when exposed by the light of self-evaluation. In addition, we all have such wounds. Typically, a person who claims not to have any fears may actually live a life dominated by repressed fear.

These repressed negative emotions and ancient psychic wounds often affect our interpersonal relationships dramatically.

In a somewhat paradoxical manner, our intense focus on following all the social activities of our friends via smartphone technology can actually cause us to neglect important interactions with those very same friends.

Another common fear directly related to the use of smartphones is that of not knowing everything that is happening in the world. We are all aware by now that media outlets are desperate for views and that most of the news items we see are trivial at best. Technology and media businesses will always present information in the most enticing manner possible.

Having realized that we have many fears, what is the solution offered by twelve-step programs to alleviate these pernicious emotions? The answer is a simple one of course. Like all aspects of a twelve-step program, we want to use the tried and true acronym KISS — Keep It Simple Stupid. We turn to our higher power for relief. We *ask* for help with our fears. If we have truly made a decision in Step Three to turn our will and our lives over, we will realize that these fears are part of our lives and that turning to our higher power for strength and guidance is essential for their removal.

We simply sincerely ask our higher power to remove our fears and allow us to fill the resulting void with some positive force.

Another common expression often heard in twelve-step programs is to "replace fear with faith."

If our request is humble and sincere, a profound effect is often felt immediately. Note that with all our defects of character consistent and sustained effort is necessary and we will continue to examine and work on these defects as we proceed through the remaining steps.

Sex Inventory

Next, in traditional twelve-step programs an inventory of our sexual conduct is begun.

Here it may be easy to see how smartphone use has affected our sex lives. Tinder? Match? Porno? Clearly, technology has radically changed the way we interact with others in sexual matters. In fact, it is obvious that technology may drive us away from actual sexual relations using pornography.

In addition, in cases where online dating apps are used, technology may depersonalize the nature of sex and cause us to view others as objects we use for sexual pleasure.

How then do we conduct a thorough inventory of our sexual conduct? The process in a traditional twelve-step program is similar to our inventories of resentments and fears.

We list the people we have harmed through our conduct, or if no other person is involved, we list the behavior with our smartphone that prevents us from having a normal sex life. Note that use of technology to please ourselves sexually can also be an indirect harm to a significant other if it causes us to neglect that person sexually.

In the second column, the actual event that caused harm to others or to ourselves is listed. In column three, we delineate the part of self that caused us to engage in the specific act. This could be a social instinct, survival instinct, or sexual instinct, for example.

In column four we reveal how we harmed another person by the feelings we created in them, and in column five the defect behind our behavior.

Here is a suggested format for taking an inventory of sexual conduct for smartphone addiction, with some examples of how inventory entries might be constructed.

Suggested Format for Inventory of Sex Conduct

Whom Did I Hurt?	What Did I Do?	What Part of Self Is Affected?	What Feelings Did I Create in Others?	Defect Causing My Part
Sandra, a girl I met on Tinder	Hooked up with her and then did not return her calls	Self-esteem Sex instinct	Shame, Insecurity	Selfishness Insecurity Lust
My Girlfriend	Used porn and then told her I was tired	Sexual instinct Insecurity Self esteem	Insecurity, Anger, Shame	Lust Insecurity Pride
Susan	Stalked her on Facebook to find out about her	Sexual instinct Insecurity Self esteem	Fear, Anger	Lust Insecurity

Sex is an area where smartphone technology can be easily used in an addictive manner. Thus, for some at least, the sex inventory as it relates to the use of the technology will reveal a clear pattern of addiction.

For others, of course, the addictive behavior may be less obvious or even repressed, which is a primary reason we do an inventory.

Pornography sites abound online and many people use these as a substitute for normal sexual relations. These sites also make it much easier to become sexually aroused and to masturbate in an uncontrolled, addictive manner.

Online dating sites and apps help facilitate an addictive use of technology and enable an addict to engage in sex as frequently as desired in some cases.

Here is another case where the technology has become so ubiquitous that it may be hard to determine what an addiction is and what is not. So where does one cross the line from normal use of technology to using it in an addictive manner where sex is concerned?

In some cases, the answer is obvious. The use of technology to facilitate a sexual addiction is similar in some respects to a gaming addiction. As described earlier, it is clear that some people are using technology for gaming in an obsessive manner. Clearly, the same is true if a person engages in sexual activity so much that the use is obsessive.

Denial of addiction is one of the primary characteristics of addiction. There is an old saying in twelve-step programs — "De Nial is not a river in Egypt." Ha-ha.

Anyway, the point is that in many cases the addict does not recognize or admit to the addiction. Even if the person sees there is a problem, they may not want to admit this for a variety of reasons.

This may be especially true for sex addiction, and perhaps particularly for women. There is still a great deal of shame and social stigma associated with sex addiction. Moreover, for a man, the use of technology via porn sites may be a shameful admission because he is substituting the machine for a real person.

Therefore, the afflicted individual may hide the behavior and not admit it to anyone, or like many addicts, only to others who are engaged in the same activities — that is, to other addicts. This is one of the common elements of many addictions that enables the addict to convince them self that they are not that bad.

Addicts will, of course, prop each other up. Specifically, if one addict associates with other addicts then the addictive behavior will become normalized. Another benefit of this perverse system of mutual support is that one can always find someone whose addiction is worse than one's own. It is common to hear things like, "At least I'm not as bad as Joe. He's really an addict." Or this, "Sue is such a slut — if I ever get that bad I'll get some help."

In addition to the review of our resentments, fears, and sex conduct, we may want to write out our life story as well. This is often a valuable exercise in self-discovery.

Recall that earlier we posed the twenty questions that were used to examine whether or not a person might be a smartphone addict. These should also be reviewed during the inventory process as an aid to self-discovery.

The 20 Questions — Are You A Smartphone Addict?

1) Does the use of your smartphone interfere with your sleeping?

2) Has your smartphone usage interfered with or affected your personal relationships?

3) Do you ever feel remorse about the way you use your smartphone?

4) Does your use of a smartphone boost or lower your self-esteem?

5) Does your use of a smartphone cause financial problems? These could be gambling, shopping, or purchasing of hardware or software products.

6) Does your smartphone use negatively affect your work?

7) Do positive or negative reinforcements from your smartphone cause you to continue to use when you know you should stop?

8) Do you lose time from school because of your use of a smartphone?

9) Has your smartphone use affected your reputation? This could be with your family, friends, school, or business.

10) Do you try to schedule or control the use of your smartphone but find that you really cannot?

11) Does good fortune drive you to use your smartphone?

12) Does misfortune compel you to use your smartphone?

13) Do you feel an obsessive urge to use your smartphone to escape feelings of boredom or loneliness?

14) Do you crave your smartphone after a short time without it?

15) Have you substituted one smartphone app for another, thinking for example that Facebook is the problem and switching to Snapchat?

16) Do you feel an urge to use your smartphone as soon as you awaken?

17) Have you ever stolen to enable your continued smartphone use?

18) Have you lied to or manipulated others to further your use of a smartphone?

19) Do you feel it would be almost impossible to live without the uncontrolled use of your smartphone?

20) Do you use a smartphone to enhance or replace normal sexual relationships, or has your use of a smartphone affected your sex life in some other way?

Once completed, our written inventory will likely contain lots of highly personal information that we will not want anyone to see. Should we keep it or destroy it? This is an individual decision, but note that we will want to keep our inventory to help us in creating our eighth step amends list. So keep it at least until then, but it may also be helpful to retain it until completing all twelve steps for reference. At that point some people keep it indefinitely, but others destroy it if they feel too compromised by having that information extant.

As revealed in our discussion of Step One, a defining element of addiction is that it creates a problem, or often a whole host of problems, in the person's life. The two elements that define the addiction are powerlessness and unmanageability.

This is one of the great benefits of a written moral inventory — it forces one who is thoroughly honest to confront their behavior and motives, and is often the first time the addict begins to clearly perceive the patterns of addiction in their life.

Without a searching and fearless written inventory of our behavior relative to smartphone technology, revealing the underlying defects of character that drive our addiction, recovery may be difficult or impossible.

STEP **FIVE**

Admitted to our higher power, to ourselves, and
to another person the exact nature of our wrongs.

Once our inventory is complete, we move on to Step Five. That
brings up a common question — "How do I know if my inventory
is complete, and I'm ready to do Step Five?"

A good perspective on working the steps, in general, is to work
the step to the best of your ability at the time you work the step.
This implies that perfection is not possible. It is easy to get stuck on
a step, especially since addicts of all types tend to be obsessive and
perfectionist anyway.

In a traditional twelve-step program, it is usually felt that the
inventory should at very least disclose all the worst parts of a person's life because recovery is truly a life or death matter.

In our case though, where we have conducted an inventory
relative to our use of smartphone tech, the answer may vary depending on our objectives. As discussed above, some people may
perform a much more detailed inventory than others may.

Note also that twelve-step programs are by their very nature intended to produce a change in the individual, and change is a process that occurs over time. So six months or a year from now after working all twelve steps, you may perform another inventory and discover additional facts.

Basically, you do the best job you can do without getting too obsessive. An old aphorism is apropos here — to thine own self be true. You know in your heart if you did a good job or not.

Having said this, it is also true that in traditional twelve-step programs one usually has access to a sponsor. Thus a sponsor can review the inventory and determine if it looks complete or not.

For our immediate purpose we may not have access to a sponsor. If we choose to work our twelve-step program with another person or persons, we can check each other's work. Hopefully as a fellowship of individuals seeking recovery from smartphone addiction develops, sponsors and others who have with experience with the steps will be available.

Therefore, what is the purpose of Step Five and how does one go about doing it?

The inventory we have created has disclosed a lot about ourselves and our internal dynamics relative to our smartphone use. It exists now in a tangible form in the universe, and one might say our addiction and our lives are out in the open for the first time ever. This may be somewhat liberating, and many will feel that there is a little additional benefit to bringing another person into the mix.

Remember that we indicated above that addicts like to deny their addiction, and not to discuss it with anyone but another addict. There is a crucial spiritual benefit to an admission of our wrongs — our "sins", in other words — to another. This has been a common practice throughout human history. Note that while twelve-step programs are not religious, many or most religious traditions contain or even require some form of confession. There is a good reason for this. We know intuitively that it is good for our soul to disclose the things we have done that we know are wrong.

The experience of twelve-step programs over time has shown that those who do not complete a thorough fourth step, and a subsequent thorough Step Five, often do not maintain recovery from their addiction, or at very least don't realize the benefits of a complete recovery.

Many addicts who have held back on these steps will eventually relapse back into active addiction. A common saying in traditional twelve-step programs is "One, two, three and out." This refers to a tendency to work the first three steps but not the subsequent ones. Meaning that the individual admits they are an addict, believes that a higher power can help, agrees to accept help from that power, but then fails to continue with the remaining steps. On the other hand, the person may skip certain steps, usually those that require the most effort, and correspondingly the greatest reward.

This is often seen in Steps Four and Five. In addition, this phenomenon is seen frequently in Steps Eight and Nine as well. Both of these sets of steps require a deep analysis of our motives and behaviors, *and* actual interaction with other human beings on an intensely personal and vulnerable level. More people who have begun working the twelve steps are lost back to active addiction on Steps Four and Five, the inventory steps, and Steps Eight and Nine, the amends steps, than at any other time in the step-working process.

As mentioned, there are also instances where an individual who has not worked all the steps may remain technically abstinent from the addictive substance or addictive behavior indefinitely, but not really change that much.

For example, a person may stay physically clean and sober, in the case of a drug addict, or not gamble, in the case of a gambling addict, but still display all the same defects of character and extreme selfishness that characterizes their addiction. In traditional twelve-step programs this may be referred to in terms such as "He's a dry drunk," in the case of alcoholism, or "She's not using but she's far from spiritually fit," in the case of an addict.

Assuming then that our inventory is complete and are ready and willing to do a thorough Step Five, how do we choose the person — the "another person" mentioned in the step — required for its successful consummation?

This can be an anxiety-provoking decision because by its very nature, the step expects us potentially to admit choices, thoughts, and actions of which we may be ashamed. Most people have some hidden secrets. The deep, dark secrets that we may have sworn we would never reveal to another person.

In traditional twelve-step programs, it is generally believed that the person should be honest, particularly in areas that are the most closely guarded secrets. Another common expression in twelve-step circles is "you're only as sick as your secrets." It is thought that holding onto these, as mentioned above, will eventually lead the individual back into active addiction. Since the result of a relapse in many addictions is death, it is a good idea to be especially careful not to hold onto any secrets.

For our purposes though, how far should a person go? Again,

it depends on the person working these steps and their ultimate goals. The type of inventory performed can be our guide here, since we should have decided earlier what we were trying to achieve and how thorough we were going to be.

Keep in mind, however, that one thing most people would agree about addiction is that it is a complex phenomenon with multiple interrelated psychological, physical, and spiritual components. This is why in twelve-step programs it is thought that only by working the steps thoroughly can a full spiritual awakening eventually be achieved.

The point is that even in our case we will want to be as thorough as possible if we are attempting to realize the full benefits of the steps to provide relief from our smartphone addiction. This is especially true if your analysis of your addiction up to this point has clearly revealed that it is having profound negative effects on your life.

Since we may be disclosing such sensitive information about ourselves, we will want to choose wisely when selecting the person to whom we convey our fifth step.

In traditional twelve-step programs, this is usually the person's sponsor. A sponsor is someone with a relatively long period of abstinence from the addictive substance or behavior who has worked the steps themselves, and then helps others with the same addiction to work through the steps. Sponsors are very common and highly encouraged in most twelve-step programs.

Therefore, the addict will usually work the fifth step with their sponsor, although this is not a requirement. Other times a priest or member of some religious tradition the addict is comfortable with can be used.

Until the fellowship of Smartphone Addicts Anonymous develops more maturity and we have more individuals who have experience working through the twelve steps for Smartphone Addiction specifically, there is another possible resource we may be able to utilize.

These are individuals in other twelve-step programs. You may know someone who is in AA, NA, OA or some other traditional program. If you believe such a person to be trustworthy and they have worked all twelve steps of their program, such a person may be an excellent choice if they are willing.

A caveat is appropriate here — be careful. Women should almost always work with other women and men with other men, especially if they are disclosing all their secrets. Also remember that by definition people in these other programs are addicts and thus sick to some extent. Recall that selfishness and dishonesty are at the core of our addiction, and this is also true for other twelve step programs. There is an old aphorism shared in twelve step programs — "Some are sicker than others." Be sure such a person is truly working a strong program, is abstinent from their addictive substance or behavior, and has integrity before you take the leap.

It is usually not a good idea to work the fifth step with a family member, because there are obvious emotional entanglements that can occur. Often these people and harms we have done to them are included in our inventory. But this is not the appropriate time to discuss the wrongs we have done to them, or to anyone else for that matter. That will come later in Steps Eight and Nine.

A close friend may be used in our case, but this would have to be someone with whom one is comfortable with the level of intimacy required. We would also want it to be someone who is not listed on the inventory, at least not for any emotionally serious matter. In any event, the person chosen must be someone who can be trusted; otherwise, the addict is not likely to be completely honest.

Another factor in selecting an individual with whom we will convey this information is to remember that by its very nature the disclosures may be troubling to some. Especially if the person is them self on your Step Four. So an important consideration is to select a person who will not be personally affected by your disclosures.

As mentioned above, a priest, rabbi, or some other religious leader may be used as well, if appropriate in your case.

One of our primary goals in working a twelve-step program is to learn how we are harming others through our addiction so that we can avoid doing so in the future. Prompting emotional turmoil in someone just to get it off our chest is not in synergy with this goal. When we get to Steps Eight and Nine we will revisit the issue of amends, and we can worry about the appropriate time and method to communicate our harms to others at that time. Right now we are on Step Five, not Step Nine.

Once the person is selected, we schedule some time and choose an appropriate location to do the step. You should be able to estimate to some degree the amount of time required, and it is best to try to get it done in one sitting so you do not have to go through it again. In a traditional twelve-step program, it is common for a very thorough fifth step to take between two and five hours, but some can take only an hour or so.

Since we may not have a dedicated sponsor to sit with us for hours in the case of smartphone addiction, it seems reasonable for now to schedule a one to two-hour block of time to complete this step.

As for location, it should be somewhere that the person who is potentially disclosing their deepest secrets feels safe and comfortable. It could be in a quiet private room in your place of residence. If the weather cooperates a park or somewhere outside works well also. Sometimes people do them in a coffee shop or some other public place as long as there is an area safe from Fifth Step eavesdroppers.

Recall that the step asks us to admit to ourselves, to our higher power, and to another human being the exact nature of our wrongs. The admission of these wrong acts and their underlying motives to our higher power is a primary objective of this step. Have we not already done that when analyzing our lives and writing out our fourth step? Again, we may ask ourselves "I have been honest with myself and God, why do I have to bring up all this embarrassing stuff to another person?"

However, the experience of twelve-step programs, and many religious and psychological traditions as well have shown clearly that confessing our wrongs to another is a profoundly life-enriching experience. Recall some of the primary defects of character in all addicts are rationalization and self-justification. So especially for addicts, who live daily with these subtly pernicious defects guiding our thinking and behavior, the complete disclosure of our sins with another is crucial to a clear perspective on our lives and addictive behavior.

Without the action of verbalizing the inventory to another human being, and at the same time our higher power, our decision to move forward in turning our life over to that power remains largely hypothetical. We perform a concrete action with the verbal release of the inventory into the universe that begins to solidify our relationship with our higher power and our fellows.

When the step is complete, we achieve a new sense of freedom and a new understanding of ourselves, our relationships with other people, and the role of our higher power in our lives.

Another result of working a comprehensive Step Four and a consequent thorough Step Five is a revealing and sometimes stark realization that we do have defects of character, that these defects have driven our addictive behavior, and that we must now be willing to accept help with these just as we did when we asked for help with our addiction. We now move on to the next indicated step, which is number Six.

STEP SIX

Were entirely ready to have our higher power
remove our defects of character.

Step Six proposes that we become "entirely ready" to work with our higher power on the removal of our "defects of character." This all sounds rather esoteric, but in reality, it is immensely practical. The real purpose of this step, and of the following Step Seven, is to improve our understanding of ourselves and the underlying causes that drive our addiction, and to strengthen our relationship with and reliance upon our higher power.

We have examined the concept of defects of character to some extent in Step Four, but now we must define these with greater precision and examine them with enhanced scrutiny.

Recall from our discussion on Step Four that selfishness was deemed to be to some extent the underlying basis of our addiction. Moreover, that this selfishness may manifest itself in a variety of disguises.

In traditional twelve-step programs, Step Six, like all the other steps, may be addressed in different ways depending on the level of thoroughness desired.

Famously in the text Alcoholics Anonymous, there is only one paragraph describing Step Six. It suggests that we ask ourselves if we will allow our higher power to remove all our defects of character, and if we find that we have a defect we want to hold onto, we ask for the willingness to seek its removal. There is no mention of writing anything down relating to Step Six or of any more involved analysis. Because of the terse verbiage, some in traditional twelve-step programs believe that a relatively unwritten quick review of known defects and an internal agreement that we are willing to have them removed is sufficient.

It is possible to work Step Six in this manner, particularly if one has a strong connection with and dependence on ones' higher power.

However, note that while Step Six — and also Step Seven — in the Alcoholics Anonymous text are notably brief, the chapters on these steps in the Twelve Steps and Twelve Traditions AA text are much more substantial. In fact, in this writers' opinion, these chapters on Steps Six and Seven are quite elegant and eloquent and convey the dramatic importance of these steps in a twelve-step program.

It is thus also common in traditional programs to work a more thorough, and sometimes much more thorough, Step Six.

A good approach is to review our Fourth Step and write out a list of one's defects of character based on the better understanding we should have of ourselves by completing Steps Four and Five. This concept of "defects of character" may seem confusing even with this better understanding, because while we touched on it in Step Four those defects were not really addressed in a highly granular manner.

Recall that Step Six asks us to be entirely ready to have all our defects of character removed. This is difficult unless we address them individually. What we will find is that we often believe we receive some benefit or "payoff" from the defect of character. Without a thorough analysis, this desire to retain the negative trait is usually repressed or masked in some way. To clarify this perhaps somewhat obtuse concept, we will need to examine defects of character and see what benefit could be obtained by retaining a defect instead of relinquishing it.

Traditional programs may list defects of character like the example below. Note that this list is the creation of this author, and you may add to or delete from it as suits your situation.

List of Defects of Character

1) Selfishness
2) Anger
3) Lust
4) Envy
5) Jealousy
6) Pride
7) Greed
8) Sloth
9) Rationalization
10) Intolerance
11) Impatience
12) Procrastination
13) Self-pity
14) Worry
15) Perfectionism

Careful readers may note that defects two through eight of these are (do not be scared off) our old friends the traditional "seven deadly sins." I mention this because a list of "defects of character" would be difficult to construct without these seven. After all, they have been around for millennia. However, I want it to be clear that our approach is non-denominational, so they are on the list but are not to be considered special in any way, or to have any particular religious significance.

One observation is that all of these defects of character are universal human qualities, exhibited throughout history and across all cultures. Another is that each has at its base a natural human instinct. Instincts are provided to us by nature to help us survive in this world. An instinct in and of itself is not bad, or a "defect of character", but a necessary feature of the way life works in the world and universe in which we exist. Instincts are based on the drive to fulfill some need that is necessary for our survival. They are thus largely biologically based and may be thought of as being "hard-wired" into our being.

For instance, lust is obviously based on sexual desire, which is necessary for the procreation of the species. Anger can be used to stimulate us to protect ourselves and our loved ones in times of danger. Worry or fear may help us to plan and thus be prepared for potential negative events in the future.

These natural instincts transform into "defects of character" when we cross some invisible threshold and the instinct is used not for its intended purpose but to satisfy our selfish and self-centered desires.

That line is invisible because our egos often do not allow us to see it, but also because although extreme examples of defects are easy to identify, most are less obvious. Especially when we are analyzing ourselves and our own motives and behaviors. These manifestations of perverse instincts at work are often easy for us to spot in others. But often only a penetrating look at ourselves will bring them to light in our own psyche.

Once we have identified these defects within ourselves, we will want to examine them carefully, and ask why we have them, and what purpose they serve.

Usually, as mentioned above, we will find that there is some underlying, often hidden, benefit we receive from the defect. This is why we must examine each defect carefully to be "entirely ready" to have it removed with the help of our higher power.

Note that we will want to analyze these defects most specifically as they apply to our use of smartphone technology, but typically, the underlying defects probably affect other parts of our lives as well.

One approach to examining our defects of character is to define a quality that might replace the defect. Usually, this is something that would be thought of as the opposite quality as the defect. This allows us to see what we might become as we cooperate further with our higher power in the removal of our defects.

By way of example, let us examine worry as a defect. What is worry? It is allowing one's mind to dwell on actual or potential problems, thereby inducing a state of anxiety and uncertainty.

Worry is a type of fear and historically has been helpful in the survival of the human species. Constantly anticipating potential negative outcomes can obviously help to avoid those outcomes.

This was a useful trait when there were lions roaming about searching for snacks.

However, today most of our worries are essentially irrational. Particularly if it is a state of mind that we are in consistently. Most people in modern societies do not have to worry about basic needs anymore. Regrettably, this is still not true for many parts of the world, but interestingly people in many less "developed" areas seem to worry less than those who have nice smartphones and a refrigerator full of food.

At this point in working our twelve-step program we should be able to realize that if we truly trusted our higher power we would not have these constant worries. This type of fear can thus be defined as a lack of faith.

Using fear then, as the defect under examination, one might ask that fear be replaced by faith. One might dwell on what a perfect faith would look like. We can ask for the strength to have faith. Sometimes it is surprising how a simple prayer can be so effective.

Where smartphone technology is concerned there exists another very specific type of fear that many users share — Fear Of Missing Out or FOMO. This term is relatively new and is thought to be one of the key drivers of addictive behavior where smartphone use is involved.

Although FOMO may be as old as humankind to some extent, prior to the advent of our connected information society there simply were not that many individual items on our radar at any given time. Technology now provides us with an essentially unlimited number of opportunities for discovering new information about past or present occurrences and possible future events.

In fact, the evidence is becoming known supporting the suspicion that capitalizing on FOMO is intentionally incorporated into the design of our information technologies. Brilliant minds are at work designing the technological solutions that dominate our lives. These designs are intended to produce certain effects that provide some business advantage for the firm. There is no evidence that this motivation for profit being the primary driver of the businesses that control smartphone technology will change anytime soon.

Technology in and of itself is an amoral force, and it appears that the development will continue indefinitely. This is perhaps not inherently good or bad, but fundamentally, an inescapable consequence of the development of technology as a sentient society advances over time.

So what is the potential benefit of retaining a defect like worry? Our minds seem to think we will lose power over a desired outcome or allow some negative outcome to occur if we do not keep it in focus in our minds. One might say that the perceived benefit is increased control over one's future.

Let's look at another defect, this time the defect of anger. This defect seems so toxic that we may find it difficult at first to find a good reason as to why we would want to keep it. But remember that the natural benefit of anger is an enhanced ability to protect ourselves or others in times of crisis. When one is angry there is a natural release of adrenaline and a physical feeling of increased power. Many people, especially men, find this feeling intoxicating, even if they do not realize this consciously. So we might say that the perceived benefit of anger is really power over others.

We will want to examine each defect of character as intently as required until we can honestly say to ourselves we would allow our higher power to remove it *completely* if we asked. If we cannot achieve this immediately, and get hung up on certain defects, we ask for the willingness to desire their removal.

At this point in our discussion, we should be sufficiently open-minded spiritually to realize that possibly our only defense against such a powerfully intelligent, constantly evolving, and over-whelmingly ubiquitous force, as smartphone technology is a higher power. This is why Step Six is the point where we begin what will become a daily process of working with our higher power on our defects. The partnership we have created will allow us to enhance our understanding of ourselves, examine the consequences of our technology use, and improve our relations with others.

A thorough analysis of our defects of character, enabling a realization of their manifestation through our selfish use of smartphone technology, and a willingness to cooperate with our higher power on their removal indicate that we are now ready to move forward and on to Step Seven.

STEP SEVEN

Humbly asked our higher power to remove
our shortcomings.

In Step Six we analyzed our defects of character and choose to cooperate with our higher power on their removal. Now in Step Seven, we make the actual request.

As we have done previously, we will want to examine some of the terminology used in the phrasing of the step, to better enable us to interpret the ultimate meaning of the step correctly. Let us start with what is meant by a shortcoming since this is the first appearance of the word in our narrative.

There has been some debate in AA and traditional twelve-step programs about what is meant in the verbiage of Step Seven by a "shortcoming," and whether it is something different from a "defect of character," as used in Step Six. Such debate is unnecessary.

When he wrote the book Alcoholics Anonymous, Bill Wilson simply wanted to use a different word in Step Seven than "defects of character." This knowledge is to some extent apocryphal, but there is much anecdotal evidence that it is true, and besides common sense tells us so. It would not make any sense to examine "defects of character" in Step Six and become willing to have them removed, and then ask for the removal of something different in Step Seven. Therefore, for our purposes "shortcoming" will be considered synonymous with "defect of character."

Since we just discussed defects of character at some length in Step Six, we should have a good understanding of what these are. In fact, the whole purpose of Step Six was to gain knowledge of these defects and be willing to have them removed. If we need to at this point, we can review Step Six and the defects of character we revealed.

Note that the step suggests that we "humbly" make this request of our higher power. The primary spiritual principle associated with Step Seven is humility. If we have worked the preceding steps to the best of our ability, we have necessarily attained some humility, even if we do not really realize this. So what is humility, and why is it so crucial to a successful consummation of Step Seven?

Let us first note that we are talking about humility and not humiliation, since in twelve-step programs the terms are often misunderstood, at least initially. To humiliate means to cause a person to become embarrassed or ashamed.

Humiliation is thus a defect of character, or a feeling related to certain defects of character like pride and shame. We can create humiliation in others or within ourselves by using smartphone technology in a selfish manner.

Humility is something completely different, and in a sense is the opposite of humiliation or at least a spiritual principle that is in strong opposition to humiliation.

In the context of many traditional religions, humility is realized through a recognition of a deity and an adherent's relationship to that deity.

Humility may be defined thusly — a balanced perspective of oneself as a human being in our higher power's universe.

This definition serves our purposes well to move forward with Step Seven. If we have worked each of the preceding steps to the best of our ability, we have gone through a process of incremental yet profound change. The simple and intuitive concept is that we can now regard ourselves in a balanced manner as inherently flawed yet uniquely beautiful manifestations of our higher power's creative ability.

We see now that we are not at the center of the universe, that we are one among many, that the well-being and feelings of others are as important as our own, and that spiritual principles can and should be the guide to our behavior.

Most importantly, we have begun to feel the power that flows into us through our higher power, and have begun to trust that this power can, with our own cooperation and efforts, transform us into the spiritually mature person we might become. We realize that the defects of character uncovered have been blocking our spiritual growth and that without the help of a higher power they will likely never change.

We can now see that being in a state of humility is a prerequisite for honestly asking our higher power to remove our defects of character.

In the preceding steps we have learned that our addictive mind denies the existence of or rationalizes these defects of character and that our addictive behavior is driven in large part through them. It follows then that some effort to remove these is necessary to recover from addiction.

Experience with the twelve steps over time indicates that the removal of these defects of character is normally not possible without the assistance of and cooperation with a higher power.

In Step One, we recognized our addictive problem and accepted in Steps Two and Three that we could not conquer the problem using our own power. In other words, we realized that to overcome addiction we required the assistance of a power greater than ourselves, were willing to accept help from that power, and agreed to work the spiritual program of action contained in the subsequent steps. Some degree of humility was required of us to achieve these realizations, even if we did not see that clearly at the time. A certain deflation of our ego was necessary even to realize a problem existed, and that we needed help from some power greater than ourselves.

A similar conceptual principle applies to Steps Six and Seven. In Step Six, we recognize clearly that we have certain defects of character that are impeding our spiritual progress, and realize that we must again cooperate with and request help from our higher power to facilitate this process.

Note that while we must be ready to have our defects completely removed, and trust that our higher power can remove them, it is likely that upon completion of Step Seven our defects will remain a part of us. As we discussed in Step Six, our defects of character are based on biological instincts that are necessary for our survival.

What we achieve through Steps Six and Seven is an ability to recognize when these instincts have overcome their bounds and morphed into defects of character, and the knowledge that our higher power can and will help with their removal, if only temporarily. The real benefit of this process is that the defects of character no longer blindly drive our addictive behavior as they once did.

Because our defects of character are such a driving force behind our addiction, and we know that we cannot recover from addiction without the help of our higher power, we should realize that we might never recover from addiction without this step.

By the time we reach Step Seven, we have a clearer conception of what humility is, or in other words, of who we are and who we might become if we are willing to follow a spiritual path. What Step Seven is really saying is that we realize we are simultaneously uniquely beautiful and tragically imperfect — like all human beings — and that we require help from our higher power to realize our spiritual goals.

Now that we have a more balanced perspective on ourselves and the root causes of our addiction, we can see clearly how our past actions, driven by our now unshrouded defects of character, have affected others. It is only with this enhanced spiritual perspective that we are now ready to move on to Step Eight, where we begin the lifelong process of examining and improving our relations with our fellow human beings.

STEP EIGHT

Made a list of all persons we had harmed, principally in connection with our smartphone use, and became willing to make amends to them all.

In traditional twelve-step programs, Steps Eight and Nine are often called the amends steps, as they are concerned with making amends to those we have harmed through our addictive behavior. It is only after we have worked the preceding seven steps that we are in a state of mind where we have developed the objectivity and clarity on ourselves and our lives that we are in any position even to list those we have harmed.

Steps Eight and Nine are concerned with how we have related to other human beings in this life, and how we may improve these relations moving forward with the knowledge we have gained on our new spiritual path. In traditional twelve-step programs, another phrase often heard regarding the amends steps is that they allow us to "clean up the wreckage of our past."

As with Step Four, it is suggested that the list constructed in Step Eight be in written or typewritten form. It is hard to keep track of something like this mentally, although we may think we can do so. It is too easy to forget some of those to whom we need to make an amends and to keep track of the amends we have made.

More importantly, recall that rationalization and justification are some of the hallmarks of all addictions. These concepts apply directly to our perception of how we may or may not have harmed someone. Once a name is on a physical list it is harder to deny the harm we caused. We can also now check off the names to whom we have made amends, and those whom we may not be able to make amends to, or should not make amends too, for a variety of reasons.

Like some of the other steps, we will want to analyze how applying Step Eight to a smartphone addiction might be different than working it on another addiction.

It is easy to see, for instance, how a drug addict or severe alcoholic might create all kinds of havoc in the lives of others. We all know that they may lie, cheat, and steal to facilitate their addiction.

Some of these harms may be rather obvious in the case of a drug addict or alcoholic:

- I stole a TV set from my friend and traded it for drugs.
- I called in sick to work and lied to my boss often when I was hungover.
- I stole money from my parents to buy drugs.
- I cheated on my husband while drunk or using.
- I got into an accident while drunk and injured someone.

It is obvious in these cases that the individual's addictive behavior caused harm to another human being. Nevertheless, while many addicts or alcoholics have clear cases like these where a direct harm was caused, even with an alcoholic or addict many of the harms are less obvious. Especially considering the aforementioned tendency of addicts to avoid contemplating the negative consequences of their addiction.

Remember that for a recovering drug addict or alcoholic the disease could not be more serious — it is fatal if left untreated. Therefore, in working a twelve-step program for these addictions, it is suggested that the person make an exhaustive list of those harmed, often like in Step Four going back through their entire life.

However, for our recovery from smartphone addiction, also like with Step Four, we will want to decide how extensive our analysis of those we have harmed and thus the list created will be.

Again this may be dependent on how serious our smartphone technology addiction is, and how seriously it has affected our lives, and thereby directly or indirectly the lives of others.

Some who believe their addiction is not too severe may want to create a simpler list of only those that their use of smartphone technology in an addictive manner has harmed.

On the other end of the spectrum, one may want to go back through his or her entire life and list all persons who they have harmed, regardless of whether the harm is related to the use of smartphone technology.

Some examples follow, but note that it is really up to the individual, and their sponsor, if they have chosen to work with one, to determine whether to utilize a more cursory or more extensive approach to working Steps Eight and Nine.

However, a caveat must be issued here — remember our old friends denial, rationalization, and justification. The addict often wants to take the easy way out, and we have proven through our addictive behavior that we are often not the best judges of what is best for ourselves or for others. Nevertheless, it is also true that at this point we have developed some degree of humility and have a more objective perspective on ourselves, so some may be able to achieve good results with a less extensive list. In any event, the real key is to actually get started on the physical production of the list and not overthink this. Right now, it is just a list.

This brings us to another common issue of confusion with Steps Eight and Nine. They are two separate steps that are to be completed in order. Thus, in Step Eight, we do not dwell too much on exactly how or when we will make a particular amends, or how the person will react, because if we do we may never put them on the list.

In Step Eight, we make a list and become willing to make amends. In Step Nine, we analyze exactly how we will make the amends, for instance, whether in person or not, and even if we will make the amends at all. An extreme instance is when a person we harmed is now deceased. In this case, we can obviously never make a direct amends, but the name and the harm we caused should go on the list anyway. There may be other ways to make amends, like through prayer. Remember the verbiage of the step is clear as to whom we put on the list — *all* persons we have harmed.

So let us make sure to keep Steps Eight and Nine separate and distinct. Presently we are in Step Eight, and so we will make a list and become willing to make an amends to each person on the list *only*. In Step Nine, we will review the nature of the amends, how and if we will make the amends, and actually make the amends if and when appropriate.

Let us begin with an example list that will apply to any approach since it will include instances where it is clear that our use of technology has harmed another.

Suggested Format for Harms List

Whom Did I Harm?	What Did I Do?	Possible Amends
My friend Susan	Posted unflattering images of her on Facebook	Contact her; say I'm sorry; Tell her I won't do it again; ask what I can do to make it right
My Mother	Lied to her about using phone at night	Contact her; say I'm sorry; Tell her I won't do it again; ask what I can do to make it right
My Wife	Used Tinder for Hookup	Need to determine if more harm would be caused, but need to become willing anyway
Co-worker Adam	Created more work for him because of my time spent on social	Face to face amends; Tell him I won't do it again; ask what I can do to make it right

We agreed earlier to work these steps to the best of our ability, so regardless of the path we choose, we should be prepared to do some serious soul searching now.

In any event, it may sometimes be difficult to ascertain those who our smartphone addiction and the subsequent defect-driven behaviors have harmed, and to whom we may owe an amends.

Because we have previously completed a thorough Step Four and Five, and have examined our defects of character carefully in Steps Six and Seven, we should have a reasonable grasp on the harms our behavior related to smartphone technology has caused others. Therefore, a good starting point for our eighth step harms list is our fourth step inventory. Remember, in our discussion on Step Four we indicated that it was a good idea to save the inventory for use in Step Eight.

As we review our inventory, we will see that naturally many of the harms we have caused to others have been listed there. However, we still want to write out every harm onto a new list for Step Eight. Just as in Step Four, the cathartic nature of the process of physically documenting these facts about ourselves is an important component of our recovery.

We will also find that since we have grown spiritually since completing the inventory, that we probably realize even more harms that may have been excluded from the inventory, whether intentionally or subconsciously. In any event, a more extensive dredging of our past relations with others is necessary in order to complete Step Eight to the best of our ability.

Note that Step Eight states that we "Made a list of all persons we had harmed, principally in connection with our smartphone use, and became willing to make amends to them all." As we have seen with many of the steps, Step Eight is multifaceted.

We have discussed at some length the idea that we should perhaps make an extensive list of those we have harmed to realize the profound effects of this step. Note though that the step contains another component, the "became willing to make amends to them all" part. What exactly does this mean?

This facet of Step Eight may seem self-evident at first, but some deeper analysis is appropriate. Note the use of the word "became," implying that the willingness mentioned is potentially the result of a process that occurs over time. This should remind us of the use of the word "came" in Step Two — "*Came* to believe that a power greater than ourselves could restore us to sanity." Remember that we recognized that Step Two expects us to possibly develop our connection with our higher power over time and not necessarily immediately.

Again, a similar — and similarly subtle — distinguishing feature of the verbiage in Step Eight is the idea that an immediate and complete willingness to make every single amends is not necessary to begin working this step. The willingness to make an amends to a specific person is not even necessary in order to place that name on the list. The idea is that the willingness to make the amends can come at some later point if we have some misgivings about a particular amends.

However, note that the step also says "... became willing to make amends to them *all*." Thus, at some point we will want to have reviewed the list, realized the harm we caused, and be willing to make amends to each person on our list.

One of the reasons this is necessary is that even though we recognize that we have caused harm through our action or inaction, it is also true that we may believe our actions were justified. This is especially true if the person we harmed has caused some harm to us. There will usually be cases in which we feel that the other individual in fact has been guilty of inflicting more harm, sometimes much more, on us than we have on them. This should again remind us of Step Four and its now insightful column four, where we focus on our faults in creating negative emotions in ourselves and others.

Again, like in Step Four, we will want to try to disregard the actions and motives of others in a situation in which we have created harm for them. This is important because in most relationships, there is a give and take, and no one is a saint. Therefore, it may be true that the other person has caused some harm to us. However, another oft-used statement from twelve-step programs is apropos here — we are trying to "Clean up our side of street."

This is why the best approach to working Step Eight is to create a list of *all* persons we have harmed. For some of these the willingness to make amends will be immediate, while in other cases we may need to reflect carefully before the willingness comes. But how can one attain willingness when it seems that the willingness is not forthcoming?

Let us remember that we agreed earlier that a primary goal in our twelve-step program was to allow our higher power to help us, since we realized that we could not defeat our addiction without help from that higher power. Each of the twelve steps has as its goal the deepening of our understanding of ourselves, our motives, our relations to others, and a more profound acceptance of the grace of our higher power. Thus, the clear and simple solution to our dilemma is to ask our higher power for the willingness until it comes.

We realized in earlier steps that we could not defeat our addiction alone, and came more and more to rely on our higher power for daily living. Now we are at a point where we try to deepen our relationships with others, and this is a crucial step in deepening our relationship with and reliance on our higher power.

In traditional twelve-step programs, another gem of an aphorism is that the higher power works through people. Alternatively, the higher power speaks through people. At least when they are in fit spiritual condition. We will have begun to realize by now in our spiritual journey that a huge component of our addiction has been the misuse of interpersonal communication to achieve our selfish goals.

Until we can recognize the harms our use of smartphone technology has caused others, and become willing to apologize sincerely for our indiscretions, the reality of the grace and power inherent in our connections with other human beings may never be realized. Only after we have painstakingly created our list and reflected sufficiently to become willing are we in the spiritual condition to make a sincere amends to those we have harmed, and thus move forward onto Step Nine.

STEP NINE

Made direct amends to such people wherever possible,
except when to do so would injure them or others.

Step Nine is a step, like Step Five, that can seem so daunting that
many people never complete it, and thus never truly realize the
full benefits of recovery from addiction. Without a comprehensive and thorough attempt to recognize and address all those we
have harmed through our addictive behavior and the making of an
amends wherever possible to these individuals and institutions, a
full spiritual awakening will likely elude us.

We can easily see why this step appears to many to be so difficult. The dredging forth of unrepented harms from the depths of
our psyches forces us to confront the worst of the tendencies that
feed our addiction. In short, it is often a painful and emotionally
demanding process.

We, of course, will worry about the response we may receive
from those we have wronged. This is especially true for those who
may not be aware of the harm, or that we were its cause.

Another set of amends that may be trying are those that contain a financial component. Let us face it; no one really likes to repay money. A common piece of advice in traditional twelve-step programs when someone complains about having to pay back money as part of a Step Nine amends is, "It's not *your* money it's *their* money." Or they may hear something like this, "You're just giving them *their* money back."

Regardless of our preconceptions and misgivings, we must persevere and move forward. We agreed to work all the steps to the best of our ability when we began this program. The restoration of a solid morality to our relationships, the relinquishment of self-ishness in interpersonal matters, and ultimately, since our higher power works at least partially through other people, the ability to perfect our connection with spirituality depend on the completion of Step Nine.

How then shall we move forward with Step Nine once we have summoned the courage to proceed? We have a thorough list that was constructed when we did Step Eight. We thought about each amends on the list and became willing to make those amends.

Step Nine requires a bit more reflection though on each instance of an amends. Timing is an important consideration when we decide how and when to make and amends in a particular situation. Recall that Step Nine tells us, "Made direct amends wherever possible, *except when to do so would injure them or others.*" We do not want to be the bull in the china shop, rushing in to hastily complete our amends so we get it over with and feel better, if the time and place are inappropriate for a certain amends.

Hindu and Buddhist traditions include an important spiritual concept, which can be summed up in the word *ahimsa*. This can be translated as *non-harming*, or *to do no harm*. The idea is that it is better to do nothing than to cause additional harm to the world.

We who are working a program of recovery from addiction have typically caused significant harm to others and to ourselves. As we have seen, this is one of the hallmarks of addictive behavior. Since selfishness and self-centeredness are some of the root causes of our addictive condition, it is not surprising that even after we have completed our Step Eight and are working Step Nine that we may still fail to see where we might cause harm through our actions.

Our job now is to make reparations for the harms we have caused, not to create additional drama and chaos in the lives of others, and thus ultimately in our own lives as well.

So we may want to initially categorize the amends into those where some harm may occur, and into those where we are reasonably sure that no additional harm will be created when we make the amends. This should be easy to do in most cases. We know in our hearts that certain people will not mind, especially if the harm we caused has not been great. We will also know, using our newfound spiritual intuition, that others are more likely to cause some harm. Many will be somewhere in the middle. For now, let us separate those harms that we are reasonably certain will cause harm and those that we are reasonably certain will not.

Now let us look at some examples that may help us to achieve this goal.

You were swiping around on a dating app. A certain particularly attractive individual caught your eye. You followed through, met the person, and had a sexual encounter. The problem is that you were married. The other person was not at the time. You had sex several times and it was clear the other person was falling in love with you, even though they knew you were married, which you did not disclose until you felt the other person was becoming too close. They were falling in love with you and said they still wanted to see you. Eventually, you sent a text informing them bluntly you never wanted to see them again. They were clearly hurt, but you did not respond and eventually communication ceased. Now it is two years later. You know that the person is now happily married.

In this case, you may not want to make a direct amends. Should you re-enter their life to apologize, dredging up the old emotional trauma and possibly endangering their current marriage? Even in a case like this, there is still room for discussion, so talk to your sponsor if you have one, a friend who has worked through the steps, or a trusted individual from another twelve-step program.

If the decision is made not to make a direct amends in a particular case, there are still ways to make amends through indirect means. Let us look at another example.

You perceived that one of your closest friends seemed to flirt with your boyfriend. You did not trust her, looked at her social media on her device without her knowledge, and never told her. This was several months ago. Your relationship with her is solid now.

In this case, you will clearly want to make an amends.

How then shall we make direct amends in the cases where we determined that such an amends would not cause further harm? Further, what is meant by a *direct* amends, anyway?

A direct amends means that we meet with the person in person, face-to-face, wherever possible. This is the preferred method for making an amends. It is too easy to make a call, and even easier to send a text, email, video, or chat. Recall also that these methods rely for many of us on the very same smartphone technology that caused the harm in the first place.

As mentioned earlier, timing is crucial in making a direct amends. We should be careful to arrange a situation where other people will not be around that may embarrass, anger, or otherwise harm the person to whom we are making our amends. This typically means being alone with the person, if only for a short time. Some amends may require more time than others, but in many cases, only a few minutes may be required. We will know intuitively for most instances whether a large amount of time is required or not.

We will usually want to give them some warning as well, unless it is someone we are very close to and the harm is not great, or we are certain the person will not get upset or require a long discussion. Meaning that we contact them and let them know that we are working a twelve-step program and are trying to make ourselves better in our interpersonal relationships. We inform them that there is something we need to speak with them about and that we owe them an amends for our behavior. We say we would like to do this in person and ask for a time that is convenient for them.

When we meet with the person, remember that our first priority is to cause no further harm. Our approach is thus non-confrontational. We are here to disclose the wrongs we committed upon the other person, and not to get into an argument over who did what to who. We reiterate that we are working a program based on our addiction and that we may not overcome that addiction unless we complete this amends step.

Then we tell them the harms we have committed, leaving nothing back. We tell them that we apologize for our bad behavior and that we will try our best not to engage in similar behavior in the future. If we owe a financial amends, we say we are willing to repay the money we owe.

An important component of Step Nine in a twelve-step program is not to simply say we are sorry, like we may have many times in the past, but also to ask the other person what we can do to make this right. We ask them if there is anything we left out, and allow them to speak.

Normally most people accept amends well. In many cases, the people realize the things we have done, or at least the general patterns of our behavior, and are happy that we have made an amends and are trying to improve our lives.

If they request that we make the financial amends we agree and make some sort of arrangements that are acceptable. Remember that no one likes to repay money, but precisely because this is so difficult, it is also a crucial step in our spiritual growth.

There may be other times where the person, either expectedly or not, reacts strongly in a negative manner. However, we are dealing with emotional and sometimes financial harm here, so it should not surprise us that someone may get upset.

In traditional twelve-step programs, one may hear in a discussion of Step Nine that "We are here to clean up our side of the street." Even if the other person really is guilty, maybe even more than us, we must remember that we are here to make our amends, and not to engage in argument. We do not say something like "I did it but it's really your fault because you did bad things to me."

The bottom line is that it should not matter if the reaction of the person to whom we are making amends is positive, negative, or somewhere in between. It is crucial that we remember that we are not to argue or act vindictively in any way but to make our amends and do our best to correct the relationship with the person we have harmed.

Nevertheless, usually when we do not fight back, as we may have in the past, an upset person will calm down and perceive our sincerity.

All this talk about yelling and angry responses may leave some with a sense of trepidation about the amends process. Do not be worried. We discuss these potential outcomes simply so you will be prepared. In reality, most amends go very well — usually far better than anticipated.

One reason we do Step Nine after the preceding eight steps is that by this time we have enhanced our spiritual being to an extent that we really are sincere in our desire to make amends for the wrongs we have committed.

Recall that Step Twelve talks about a "spiritual awakening as the result of these steps." If we have been thorough up to this point in our step work, we will have begun to sense the flow of spirit into ourselves. We are now almost three-fourths of the way through the twelve steps, and the purpose of the steps is to produce positive change in us and thus in our relations with others, and with our higher power.

By now fear, anger, and other defects of character that dominated our lives and drove our addictive behavior will be less severe. We will realize how our addictive use of technology has harmed others and will want to find ways to use our technology in a less selfish and self-centered manner.

Once we have completed Step Nine, we will have a new appreciation of the spiritual beauty inherent in interpersonal relationships, a deeper and more profound connection with our higher power, and a better and more complete understanding of ourselves and our place in this universe. We will now want to preserve this fresh and wonderful perspective, and thus move on to Step Ten, which will give us the tools and direction to maintain our spiritual condition on a daily basis.

STEP **TEN**

Continued to take personal inventory, with a
special emphasis on our use of smartphones,
and when we were wrong promptly admitted it.

Now that we have completed the first nine steps of our program
of recovery from smartphone addiction, we may sense that we are
near the end of our journey. In fact, while much of the initial work
— and certainly the most difficult work — has been completed, we
are now on a spiritual path of living that requires consistent effort
to maintain.

In traditional twelve-step programs Steps Ten, Eleven, and
Twelve are sometimes referred to as "the maintenance steps." What
does this mean and why would we need to "maintain" our recovery?

One might think that having completed all this difficult personal work, thereby establishing a reliance on our higher power, an
understanding of ourselves, and our relations to others, that we are
done. After all, we should by now realize that with the guidance of
our higher power we no longer need to be enslaved by our technology, and probably feel at least somewhat empowered in this respect.

Recall, however, that some of the primary characteristics of most traditional addictions are that they are considered to be chronic, progressive, incurable, and eventually fatal if left untreated.

Chronic may be defined as persisting for a long period, difficult to eradicate, and reoccurring. A definition of progressive in our context is a disease that gets continuously worse over time. Incurable of course means that there is no known cure — the disease can never be permanently eradicated in the afflicted individual.

Note that there are diseases other than addiction that fit the above definition. Some of these are treatable and can be controlled, while others are not. We could easily come up with a list of physical and even psychological conditions, which can be treated and brought under control with particular treatments, and other diseases that unfortunately cannot be treated.

Thankfully for us, addiction is thought to be in the former category.

This disease concept is one of the key features of traditional twelve-step programs, originating primarily with Alcoholics Anonymous. The idea is that while the underlying disease of alcoholism is chronic, progressive, incurable, and eventually fatal if left untreated, at the same time the afflicted individual can live a normal life indefinitely if they have a spiritual awakening and then follow a few simple rules on a continuous basis.

This means that we can recover from the addiction, but the recovery requires some effort — some "treatment" if you will — to establish and maintain.

As we have discussed previously, in traditional chemical addictions like alcoholism or drug addiction, part of the "treatment" included in a twelve-step approach is complete abstinence from the addictive substance. There are other treatment models for these addictions that believe complete abstinence is not always necessary for recovery. However, Narcotics Anonymous and Cocaine Anonymous for drug addiction, and Alcoholics Anonymous for alcoholism, all suggest the person not drink or use drugs entirely in order to establish a successful recovery.

In other traditional twelve-step programs, complete abstinence may also be the goal. In Gamblers Anonymous, for instance, the afflicted person is advised to stop gambling completely.

In other cases, though, it is unreasonable to achieve or even suggest complete abstinence. In the twelve-step program Sex Addicts Anonymous, for example, the person is encouraged not to engage in addictive sexual behavior but becoming celibate for the rest of their life is not necessarily part of the program.

As we have discussed previously, in general, it is unrealistic in most cases to believe that a person in contemporary society can achieve complete abstinence from the use of smartphone technology. This is because the use of smartphone technology is so thoroughly interwoven into our everyday existence. A more complete analysis of abstinence as it relates to smartphone addiction is provided later in this text.

Therefore, to reiterate our goal is to control our use of smartphone technology, especially by not harming others through its selfish use. Nevertheless, we still suggest that our smartphone addiction fits our definition of a disease that is chronic, progressive, and incurable. As we have seen, while it may seem extreme, in certain cases the "eventually fatal if left untreated" part of the definition applies as well.

Thus, we can perceive smartphone addiction as a disease where moderation and a balanced usage of the addictive technology is a reasonable objective and the key to recovery, and realize our twelve-step program is the means to achieve this goal.

Thus, having said all that, we are back to the question as to why we need to "maintain" our recovery.

One reason is that as we have discovered in working the steps, especially Steps Four through Nine, that we have defects of character which we have identified, and that these drive our addictive behavior and cause us to harm others by using our technology in a selfish manner.

At this point in our program, fresh from the successful completion of Step Nine, these defects, the way they manifest themselves in our lives, and the way they block us from our fellows and our higher power may seem obvious.

However, the experience of traditional twelve-step programs is that this clear and humble perspective does not last long. At least without continued action.

Some of the key features in traditional twelve-step programs that are thought to allow a person to maintain recovery are the emphasis on daily inventory, which we focus on here in Step Ten, improving our spiritual contact, which we cover in Step Eleven, and trying to help others, the focus of Step Twelve.

This is true for all traditional twelve-step programs, from Alcoholics Anonymous to Narcotics Anonymous, from Gamblers Anonymous to Sex Addicts Anonymous, and even in Al-Anon, where the twelve steps are applied to the issue of addictive codependence of a loved one on the actual addicted individual.

Sometimes we forget that we did not necessarily become addicted to our smartphones overnight. Our patterns of addictive behavior and thinking typically develop over time, sometimes many years. The thoughts and habits of a lifetime, or any long period, do not change permanently overnight, even if we may think they have.

It should not be surprising then that retaining our new perspective requires maintaining that new perspective. This means more action and effort.

Recall that defects of character are based on natural instincts, and these instincts are still present in us as human beings and always will be. Experience shows that the defects of character we have identified are also still present in our lives. Without a daily inventory of our motives and behavior, we tend to drift back into allowing these defects to dominate our lives.

Our selfish and self-centered behavior returns, and our thinking changes accordingly. The fear and anger that drive us are no longer so apparent and we tend to creep back into rationalization and justification of our addictive behavior.

How then shall we prevent this? We have worked hard to get to this point in our recovery and now realize, often to our consternation, that more effort is involved. It may seem easier to fall back into our old ways, but this is where we must reenergize ourselves by remembering our commitment to doing whatever was necessary to recover from our addiction.

Fortunately, the solution at this point is relatively easy. The key is that if we analyze ourselves and our motives and behavior every day, we will not create lots of complicated new wreckage like we did in the past that requires a huge amount of effort to clean up.

Step Ten is essentially an examination of our actions and motives during the day. We will see that Step Ten really is worked daily in conjunction with Step Eleven, and then Step Twelve, and that the three steps together form an unshakeable synergistic methodology for daily living according to spiritual principles.

The actual working of Step Ten asks us to take an inventory of our day. Before retiring at night, we can review our day. We will want to note especially where any defects of character caused us to act in a selfish manner concerning our use of smartphone technology.

We may have become angry or fearful when access to our smartphone was threatened. We may have texted while driving and almost gotten into an accident, or perhaps even gotten into an accident because of our smartphone. We may have ignored a friend in need.

In reviewing our day, we will also want to take note of good actions or thoughts as well. We may have followed through on our commitment to not text while driving for the entire day. We may have not allowed our smartphone use to keep us from actual interpersonal relations with other human beings.

We thus see that the personal inventory includes a balanced analysis of our day and not simply a focus on the things we did that were wrong.

Another component of taking daily inventory, in addition to the nightly one covered above, is to monitor our behavior and motives throughout the day. If we can do this often, we can sidestep bad behavior or selfish use of our smartphone technology before it happens.

We also remember that we now have a relationship with our higher power and know that we have tapped into a source of power that can help us if we ask. Therefore, we cooperate with our higher power in the inventory process, asking for help when necessary, or in moments when we feel weak or uncertain.

We also note that the step specifically states that we agreed that "when we were wrong (we) promptly admitted it." This is an important component of Step Ten, and of our ongoing recovery. Having just worked Steps Eight and Nine, we realize how our selfish and self-centered addictive behavior has harmed others and have become comfortable with the knowledge that we must make amends whenever appropriate if we are to stay in recovery.

Thus, when we have harmed someone during the day through our selfish motives and behavior, we can apologize to them as soon as possible. We may be able to make amends immediately, but as with Step Nine, we will be careful with our timing so that we do not cause more harm.

At other times, we may not realize we owe an amends until we review our day in the evening. In the heat of the moment, the selfish behavior may not be apparent. At the time we take our daily inventory, we will always want to be relaxed and quiet if possible. In this state, we are more likely to achieve a balanced and objective perspective on our actions and motives that day.

If we find we owe an amends we plan for the time to make the amends, being careful as always of the timing and cognizant of not creating further harm.

Once we have carefully reviewed our day, not forgetting to note the good actions and motives as well as the bad, we can sleep in good conscience. We will also remember to thank our higher power for help in maintaining our recovery for that day, which is an integral component of our next step, Step Eleven, where we strengthen our relationship with and reliance on our higher power.

STEP ELEVEN

Sought through prayer and meditation to improve
our conscious contact with our Higher Power,
praying only for knowledge of His or Her will for us
and the power to carry that out.

Once we have reached Step Eleven we will by now have established an increasingly intimate connection with our higher power and the beginning of an understanding that can strengthen indefinitely, providing we are willing to maintain that relationship with certain simple actions.

Step Eleven suggests that we utilize the synergistic spiritual practices of prayer and meditation to improve our conscious contact with our higher power and that the object of these efforts be to focus only on knowledge of our higher powers will for us and for the necessary power to manifest that will into reality.

The verbiage of this step comprises a veritable cornucopia of spiritual terminology, so let us spend a little time at first examining some of the primary concepts at play here.

Higher Power

We have examined the concept of a higher power throughout our analysis of the steps thus far, but since this concept is so crucial to Step Eleven, we will take a closer look, keeping in mind what we have learned about our higher power through working the preceding ten steps.

One of the absolute core precepts of any twelve-step program is the idea that the individual working the program can, and should in most cases, develop their own conception and understanding of a higher power.

As we have discussed, the higher power can be *any* power that is greater than the individual. Initially at least this power need not be clearly defined or understood. A common piece of wisdom conveyed to newcomers in a twelve-step program might go something like this — "Your higher power can be anything as long as it's not you."

As we have learned, however, the key concept of any twelve-step program is the idea that because of one's personal powerlessness over the addiction, this higher power can and will be able to relieve one of the addiction, if the individual works the steps and relies on that power.

Another fundamental idea is that through working the steps the afflicted individual over time will establish an increasingly personal connection and relationship with that power. Thus, by Step Eleven we realize not only that our higher power can relieve us of our addiction, but that he or she has done so up to this point. We will also have achieved a new sense of spiritual purpose and a relinquishment of some of the selfishness that characterized our addictive behavior.

By now, we will understand intellectually and intuitively that our higher power can stand between our smartphone technology and us, and that technology need not control us as it has. We will see that spiritual reality truly consists of the timelessness and universality of correct ethical principles of conduct and unconditional compassion for other human beings and that this correct perspective on spirituality has been blocked through a selfish attachment to the potentially harmful forces of smartphone technology.

One of the primary mechanisms for achieving this perspective, if we have worked the steps to this point to the best of our ability, has been prayer. We will have necessarily engaged in prayer conscientiously on a regular basis to achieve our fresh and joyful attitude towards smartphone technology and our fellows. Let us now look deeper into prayer.

Prayer

We may define prayer as an intentional action that seeks to establish communication with a spiritual entity, either as a request for something desired or as an expression of gratitude for something received.

The request may be for guidance, for knowledge, for the well-being of oneself or another, but might also be for material possessions, for success in some endeavor, or for life itself. An expression of gratitude could be for any of these things as well, or a general conveyance of thanks for all blessings received.

Note of course that some of the above are selfish requests, and some are not. One of our primary goals in Step Eleven and of our twelve-step program in general, is to utilize prayer for non-selfish ends. Thus, the phrase "praying only for knowledge of our higher powers' will for us and the power to carry that out."

Prayer is our primary means of contact with our higher power and is perhaps our first and ultimate line of defense against using our smartphone technology in a selfish manner.

We might say something like this:

My higher power, help me to realize that my smartphone can be a tool that can enhance my life and allow me to be of greater service in your world. Help me to relinquish my obsessive attachment to smartphone use, and to understand that compassion for and contact with other human beings are key purposes for my existence in this physical form in your universe.

As mentioned above, another form of prayer is one of gratitude. In this type of prayer, we thank our higher power for something specific, or perhaps proffer a sense of general gratitude for all blessings we have received.

To implement a prayer of gratitude one could try this example:

Dear Higher Power, I am thankful for all the blessings you have bestowed upon me and those I love.

Another prayer is the kind we might use in a situation where we are tempted to use our smartphone technology when we know we should not.

Some might wonder if this use of prayer for guidance on a particular event reflects the stated intent of the step that is, "praying only for knowledge of his will for us and the power to carry the out." The answer is "yes" if we structure the prayer appropriately and with proper intent.

Perhaps we could offer a prayer like the following:

Higher Power, please help me in this situation to make the right choice that places me in a position of maximum usefulness to you and others.

Meditation

Step Eleven also specifically mentions meditation as a means we can utilize to establish contact with our higher power.

There is a sometimes-lively debate in recovery concerning what exactly was meant in the original use of this word in the twelve steps. This is because in 1939 when the twelve steps were first published in the book Alcoholics Anonymous, meditation was not as popular as it is today. Eastern meditation techniques like mantras, breathing, seating positions, and all the other things we think of when we say mediation today were not common knowledge then.

So many people question whether our current perspectives on meditation match those of the founders of AA.

Some think it is likely that they regarded mediation as a time of quiet reflection, a calming of the mind in order to hear the silent voice of one's higher power. One of the aphorisms heard in twelve-step meetings is, "Prayer is talking to your higher power, and meditation is listening."

There is no need for debate. The founders are known to have been amazingly open-minded, in particular to alternative ideas on spirituality, and I believe we can use a broad definition of meditation that will encompass multiple perspectives.

My definition of meditation is a deliberate attempt to focus mental energies and calm one's body and mind in order to achieve an increased state of spiritual awareness.

Thus, simple quiet reflection, active listening for the voice of a higher power, repeating a formal mantra, disciplined breathing, less disciplined breathing, and many others, are all forms of meditation. The key is — at least for meditation specifically related to Step Eleven — that the *intention* behind the meditative action we take is to establish and improve our conscious contact with our higher power.

Our understanding of meditation and its spiritual benefits will increase in proportion to the time and effort we spend engaging in this potentially life-changing activity. In other words, like prayer, exercise, or eating well, one actually has to engage in meditation to achieve any of the benefits of meditation.

As we have discovered in the preceding steps, obtaining the spiritual rewards of any step requires that we work the step to the best of our ability.

An oft-heard phrase in many spiritual disciplines that include meditation is that of meditation as a *practice*. Thus, we may hear phrases like "the practice of meditation," or "I'm going to meditation practice." This tells us something about meditation, informing us that it is a skill that can be perfected through repetitive practice and study.

Assuming that we now agree meditation is an important and perhaps crucial component of our spiritual program, we will want to know how to meditate. Many fantastic books, videos, apps, podcasts, and blogs are available that specifically focus on this popular activity. An understanding of what techniques to use will occur over time with repeated practice and study. However, where to begin now?

The answer is almost too simple. To get started with meditation one need only sit with intention and breathe.

Almost all meditative schools include a focus on the breath. Our breath fulfills the most immediate and fundamental need for any human being, that of air flowing into and out of our body, and yet it is one that we usually ignore, to some extent *because* of its perpetual and ubiquitous nature.

If we allow it, the breath ties us to our body and to the present moment, which is to say to reality itself. Focusing on the breath calms us, placing us in a mental and physiological state that allows us to activate the higher portions of our consciousness.

This physical and psychological tranquility places us in a position in which our defects of character subside from consciousness and have less control over our thoughts and physiology. In a sense, this meditative state can be perceived as allowing for the removal of the obstacles that exist in consciousness, blocking our conscious contact with our higher power. This state allows us to attain a higher level of spiritual awareness, and to clear and magnify a channel of communication between our higher power and us.

Conscious Contact

This brings us to another key concept of Step Eleven, that of *conscious contact*. The step suggests that we use the twin tools of prayer and meditation, discussed above at some length, to *improve* our conscious contact with our higher power.

The phrase conscious contact almost defines itself, but this apparent simplicity requires examination anyway. Consciousness can be defined as a state of awareness or having knowledge of something. In Step Eleven, that awareness or knowledge is that of contact, specifically with one's higher power.

Almost all spiritual and religious traditions place great importance on the idea of contact with a higher power. We can see why this is so important by examining what it means not to have that contact.

One of the key conceptual axioms in many traditions is that all or most human problems are due to a lack of contact with whatever higher power may exist since that power is the source of truth in life.

A good way to perceive a lack of contact with anything is as a *separation* from that thing. At times, this is a conscious separation, while at other times it may be unintentional.

Most people feel some intuitive connection with a higher power at some point in their lives. A number of causes can enhance or deplete this connection. Sometimes it is an issue with organized religion, or some traumatic event in our lives, or an intellectual defiance. As anyone can see, there are complex and innumerable events that can influence an individual's spiritual development.

In eastern spiritual traditions, it is thought that suffering is based on a lack of understanding of our true nature. When an individual forgets that her true source is rooted in eternity and infinity, separation from the source of truth and power results, and from this separation all suffering occurs.

The essence of most religious traditions is in-fact some sort of connection, or contact, with the source of truth, goodness, love, and power that governs our existence. This ultimate source is often defined and perceived differently, but in the final analysis, there is more commonality in spiritual concepts than the opposition.

It is easy to see how a person who is severely addicted to drugs or alcohol might lose conscious contact with a higher power. That is, to experience separation from the source of truth and power in life.

Another example of the development of separation is in an attachment to material things. As the desire for material objects and wealth grows stronger, it can dominate a life until that person is effectively in separation from the ultimate source of what is ethically correct and important in life.

We have seen that in all addictions one of the defining and common characteristics is the effect the addiction has on the spiritual condition of the afflicted individual.

We can now see how our addictive smartphone use might cause a separation from our higher power. The unnatural nature of an obsessive connection with a smartphone is in some ways directly antithetical to a connection with spiritual reality.

Our addiction to smartphone technology is fundamentally similar to other addictions in terms of how the addiction creates a separation from the source of spiritual power in our lives.

We now have our two primary tools for connection — or, if you wish, the reduction of separation — with our higher power. The first is prayer — we can see from our examination of prayer that this spiritual activity is a clear form of conscious contact. The other is meditation — our analysis of meditation also reviewed how that activity placed us in conscious contact with our higher power. Our goal now is to continue to use these two techniques to improve that contact.

Our Higher Power's Will for Us

Step Eleven also suggests that we seek our higher powers will for us, and the power to carry that out. A common quandary in traditional twelve-step programs is how to distinguish one's own will from that of ones' higher power, and this is certainly true for us as well.

A sponsor in a twelve-step program might say something like "If you're thinking about helping someone else it's probably God's will. If you're thinking about helping yourself it probably isn't."

As with many such comments, there is an important truth hidden beneath the seemingly black and white message.

As we have previously established, we know that some of the characteristics of addiction are rationalization and justification. Especially early in our recovery, and especially if we *are* thinking about something for ourselves, we must be very careful about distinguishing God's will from our own.

This is one reason that a fellowship of other individuals in recovery from the same addiction is an important and core element of traditional twelve-step programs. It is too easy for us to justify almost any thought or behavior. Remember that selfishness and self-centeredness are at the core of our addiction.

Running our bright ideas past a sponsor, another member of our fellowship, or at least someone we trust to tell us the truth, will help us to distinguish God's will from our own. Over time, as we improve our conscious contact with our higher power through prayer and meditation, we will gain a deep and profound connection that will enable us intuitively to comprehend situations that once confused us.

The preceding ten steps have made us aware of the problem and of the solution. We realize now that the solution is a spiritual one, and that we must maintain our spiritual condition through effort.

Step Eleven allows us to connect and cooperate with our higher power to live well on a daily basis, without allowing our smartphone use to create separation between us and Him or Her.

Having gained this new and wonderful perspective on ourselves, our relationships with others, and our connection with our higher power, we are now in a position to help other smartphone addicts achieve a spiritual awakening as well, which is the primary focus of Step Twelve.

STEP TWELVE

Having had a spiritual awakening as the result of these steps, we tried to carry this message to other smartphone addicts, and to practice these principles in all our affairs.

Now that we have worked through the first eleven steps to the best of our ability, we find ourselves at the last step in our program of recovery from smartphone addiction.

In traditional twelve-step programs, Step Twelve is usually conceived as consisting of three related but distinct components. Commas in the step verbiage separate these components. Moreover, although these elements comprise distinct thoughts and courses of action, they work together to form a single synergistic spiritual solution as well.

The first of these components is contained in the phrase "Having had a spiritual awakening as the result of these steps." Next, we find another element in the phrase, "We tried to carry this message to other smartphone addicts." The third and final facet is contained in the words, "And to practice these principles in all our affairs."

Let us examine each of these in turn, and then see how they beautifully integrate to comprise our final step of action in recovery.

Spiritual Awakening

Although we have touched upon it before, we now want to look more carefully at the concept of spiritual awakening. What is a spiritual awakening and what does it mean when someone has one?

We have utilized the word spiritual throughout this work and the concept is fundamental to all twelve-step programs and to ours in particular. One perspective is that spiritual means that which is related to the human spirit or soul, as opposed to matters related to material or physical things.

The soul or spirit may be considered as the connection point or bridge between a human being and a divine one. This point of contact between our higher power and us is not something that can be physically touched or defined scientifically, and can only be realized through faith and action.

As we have discussed previously, spirituality may be defined as an attempt to cooperate with God. Spirituality depends on the connection point between us and God — the soul or spirit — being clear and free of obstacles. As we have seen, we have built up dense barriers in the form of defects of character that have impeded our ability to experience spiritual reality.

Therefore, in a sense, our work up until now has served to clear the channel of connection to our higher power, allowing a message of love and truth to flow into us, whereas in the past we were incapable of receiving this flow in an unadulterated manner.

Thus, we can now perceive why we use the term awakening.

To awaken means to rouse something from sleep. We may perceive it as bringing something into awareness or back to consciousness. The key here is that the awakened entity, whether a hibernating bear or the spirituality of a recovering smartphone addict, already exists but had been dormant.

Note that the step says, "Having had a spiritual awakening as the result of these steps." The implication here is that this spiritual awakening occurs if and only if the recovering addict works through the preceding eleven steps.

So the awakening of our spirituality can be seen as bringing back to life a natural component of our being that had been suppressed in our active addiction.

Perhaps we may then simply perceive a spiritual awakening as a realization of our connection with God as the source of love, power, and guidance in our lives, and thus the solution to our smartphone addiction.

Recall that we used the word cooperation in defining spirituality. Part of cooperation with God, and thus part of spirituality, is to act on the message of love and truth we have received.

This thought serves to transition us into the second component of Step Twelve, where we reach out to our fellow sufferers who may not have knowledge of our simple and effective solution to the challenge of smartphone addiction.

Carrying the Message

The verbiage of the second of the three elements of Step Twelve is, "We tried to carry this message to other smartphone addicts."

Note that the step uses the term "message." We intuitively

understand what a message is, but let us examine this concept a bit more closely.

So what is "this message," in our case? Quite simply this message is the idea that recovery from our addiction is possible, that we have a specific and effective solution in the steps, that we are addicts too and the solution worked for us, and that the solution continues to work in our lives on a daily basis.

However, this idea of carrying the message is crucial to and is in fact one of the foundational principles in twelve-step programs. If we examine the history of Alcoholics Anonymous, we will understand just how important this idea is for recovery in twelve-step programs.

Bill Wilson, the co-founder of Alcoholics Anonymous and primary author of the book Alcoholics Anonymous, realized almost immediately when he achieved permanent sobriety on December 10, 1934, that he wanted to pass on the spiritual experience he had and reach out personally to other alcoholics.

His understanding was more intuitive and his method for reaching out different from what would be his later perception. He spent a significant amount of time in the next several months personally trying to help other alcoholics.

Famously, as it turned out, not one of them stayed sober. Discouraged at one point, he said to his wife and closest supporter and confidante, Lois Wilson, "None of these men stayed sober." In a crucial moment in the history of twelve-step programs, Lois conveyed a clear and enlightened perspective to Bill with this response, "You stayed sober, Bill." This led him to the epiphany that perhaps the action of trying to work with other alcoholics had been instrumental in keeping him sober.

Also important in changing his thinking regarding this concept of carrying the message was a discussion around this same time with Dr. William Silkworth, a figure who was another important influence on the development of AA. Dr. Silkworth was Director of the Charles B. Towns Hospital for Drug and Alcohol Addictions in New York City in the 1930s, and treated Bill Wilson on three separate occasions.

In an important moment in twelve-step history, Bill described the approach he was using with the men he had tried to get sober. Dr. Silkworth believed that Bill was in a sense preaching and that this was one reason why he was not successful.

He suggested that Bill describe his experience as an alcoholic and what had happened to him, rather than preaching. This leads to what is regarded in twelve-step programs as the concept of identification. That is, the fact that one addict identifies with another and breaks down barriers that have kept them from hearing the message from anyone else. Meaning that in many cases experience shows that *only* another addict can carry an effective message of recovery to another.

These two perspectives, from Lois that working with others was crucial to maintaining his own sobriety, and from Dr. Silkworth of conveying one's own personal experience — along with Bill's sense of duty and passion for helping others — led to the perspective on recovery Bill had when he travelled to Akron, Ohio on a business trip in May of 1935.

Eventually his business deal had fallen apart and feeling down on his luck he stood in the lobby of the Mayflower Hotel. At one end of the lobby, he could see and hear the happy crowd in a festive bar. At the other end of the lobby was a payphone. He thought about having just one drink, and realized he was on thin ice.

He realized if he drank, he would not only get drunk and destroy his own life, but that other alcoholics would not receive his message of recovery, which was now more mature as described above.

In one of the foundational moments in the history of Alcoholics Anonymous, and thus of twelve-step programs in general, Bill Wilson turned and walked to the payphone instead of going into the bar. There was also a directory of churches near the payphone, a common feature in that era. He made a series of calls to church ministers, explaining his situation and asking if they knew of any alcoholics he might help.

Eventually, he was given the name of Henrietta Seiberling, a daughter-in-law of the founder of the Goodyear Tire Company. Though not an alcoholic herself, she was a member of The Oxford Group in Akron, which was very popular there at that time. Henrietta thought immediately of an Oxford Group member who was struggling with alcoholism and gave Bill the phone number to reach Dr. Bob Smith.

Bill and Dr. Bob met two days later in the gatehouse at the Seiberling mansion. Interestingly, the gatehouse still stands and is a National Historic Landmark because it was the location of the initial meeting of the co-founders of Alcoholics Anonymous.

At the meeting, Bill and Dr. Bob met for five hours. Dr. Bob described it best in his story from the book Alcoholics Anonymous — "He was the first person I had ever met who understood what I was going through on the basis of actual personal experience."

Dr. Bob achieved permanent sobriety on June 10, 1935, which is now regarded as the birthdate of Alcoholics Anonymous.

Recall that this was years before the twelve steps were first created in 1939. There was no AA book or any AA groups. At this time, they attended Oxford Group meetings and used the Oxford Group methodology.

Nevertheless, they had an understanding of the importance of carrying the message of recovery through their personal experience.

The two immediately realized that they needed to get busy. They began to search out other alcoholics in need. They were frustrated for a while but persevered. They eventually found Bill Dotson, who became AA Number Three, and who stayed sober permanently. This validated their approach and they continued very actively to work with other alcoholics, Bill in New York after his return there and Dr. Bob in Akron.

This idea of service to others and specifically trying to carry the message to others with the same addiction is also fundamental to all other twelve-step programs of recovery.

Thus, we can see that this is also of crucial importance to our program of recovery from smartphone addiction and that our continued recovery and happy existence may depend on our actions in this area.

Part of our spiritual awakening is the realization that what we have received is a gift. A gift of grace, from our higher power, sufficient to bring about our recovery.

Grace may be considered as unmerited divine assistance — something received but unearned. The reason this is considered a proper perspective is that many who have the same addiction never get the chance to recover. They are no more or less deserving than those who somehow get to experience recovery. There is also no clear explanation as to why we experienced a moment of clarity in which we saw that we were powerless and needed help, while others did not.

Therefore, we also realize that at least one of the reasons we have received this gift of grace is that we are now in a position to carry the message of an effective solution to others.

Practice These Principles

Now we analyze the third element of Step Twelve, the phrase "And to practice these principles in all our affairs."

This may appear to be a daunting task, and we may not comprehend precisely what the statement means. Let us take a closer look at the meaning of this component of Step Twelve.

Here, we will want to examine some definitions again in order to better understand the intended meaning.

In a Step Twelve context, we might initially consider practice as meaning the repeated attempts at an activity in order to improve a skill, like practicing on a piano. It is true that as we apply ourselves to working our spiritual program on a daily basis that we get better at it, but this is a side effect in a sense, and I do not believe this is the intended meaning of the word in this context.

Practice here means the actual application or use of an idea rather than theorizing about the application or use of an idea. An example of this definition would be the practice of medicine after medical school.

Therefore, in our case, we want actually to use the spiritual principles we have learned in our twelve-step journey thus far rather than sit around and think about them.

Next, we want to know what is meant by the phrase "these principles." We mean by this the various spiritual principles inherent in our discussion of the steps thus far.

Let us first consider the meaning of the word principle in this context. We may define principle as a fundamental truth that acts as the foundation for a system of belief.

Each step in our program of recovery actually contains a number of spiritual principles. The idea that our twelve-step program is really intended to convey or be perceived as a set of spiritual principles is a profound thought and sometimes difficult to comprehend at first.

Before working our twelve-step program of recovery, we based our actions on momentary and unethical selfish desires rather than on timeless and correct spiritual principles.

Once we have worked through all twelve-steps to the best of our ability our thoughts and actions will be based on different principles than we utilized prior to our recovery work.

The specific principles to which we are referring are not explicitly spelled out in Step Twelve. This is also true for any of the other eleven steps except perhaps Step Seven, which explicitly mentions the spiritual principle of humility in its verbiage.

However, based on our work thus far if asked we should immediately realize a number of spiritual principles that we now utilize as the basis of our actions. These might include honesty, faith, forgiveness, humility, love, and service.

Some have attempted to isolate a single spiritual tradition that is the basis of each step. A list of principles and their corresponding step has circulated in AA for many years.

It is not completely clear where this list originated, and AA does not officially sanction it. Alcoholics Anonymous, as far as this author knows, has no such officially sanctioned list of spiritual principles associated with the twelve steps of Alcoholics Anonymous. It is included here for the sake of completeness.

The idea is that each step has at its core one primary spiritual principle. Here is one such list, perhaps the most popular, which is associated with the twelve steps of Alcoholics Anonymous. To reiterate, Alcoholics Anonymous does not sanction this list.

The Spiritual Principles of the Twelve Steps
One Historical List

Step 1 — Honesty

Step 2 — Hope

Step 3 — Faith

Step 4 — Courage

Step 5 — Integrity

Step 6 — Willingness

Step 7 — Humility

Step 8 — Love

Step 9 — Discipline

Step 10 — Patience

Step 11 — Awareness

Step 12 — Service

As mentioned above, in reality, each step comprises multiple spiritual principles. It is a normal human tendency to simplify and attempting to assign one principle to each step is an example of this. Here is another list assigning pertinent spiritual principles to the Twelve Steps for Smartphone Addiction. Note that this is a construction of the author. Others may find various principles in their interpretation of the steps.

The Spiritual Principles of the Twelve Steps for Smartphone Addiction

Step 1 — Surrender, Honesty

Step 2 — Open-mindedness, Hope

Step 3 — Willingness, Faith

Step 4 — Honesty, Courage

Step 5 — Integrity, Acceptance

Step 6 — Introspection, Willingness

Step 7 — Humility

Step 8 — Forgiveness, Love

Step 9 — Discipline

Step 10 — Gratitude, Patience, Forgiveness

Step 11 — Awareness, Faith

Step 12 — Love and Service

It may seem difficult or even impossible to be able to incorporate all these principles in all our affairs. Moreover, it is, because we are human. Recall though that in our program of recovery from addiction we strive for consistent spiritual improvement, not spiritual perfection.

Remember that part of the spiritual principle of humility is to know that we are imperfect. Therefore, we try our best on a daily basis to think and act using our twelve-step principles as our guide.

Thankfully, Steps Ten and Eleven are our allies in this endeavor. If we are working these steps each day, to some extent our ability to practice these principles in all our affairs becomes almost second nature.

Step Twelve allows us to see that our program of recovery from smartphone addiction truly is a set of spiritual principles through which we receive sustained recovery from our addiction, upon which we can ethically base our thoughts and actions, and which we can pass on to fellow addicts as a possible new way of life.

A WAY OF LIFE

Now that we have worked through all of the twelve steps for smartphone addiction, thereby having experienced the promised spiritual awakening, we shall have begun to realize that a twelve-step program is, in reality, a way of life.

One of the key concepts of our twelve-step perspective on addiction is that addiction is incurable and progressive. Meaning as we have seen through our discussions and our analysis of our own addiction through the twelve-step process, that our addiction may be controlled but not eliminated and if not controlled becomes progressively worse over time.

Thus, a core precept at the heart of all twelve-step programs is the ongoing nature of recovery from addiction, and the necessity of continuous maintenance of that recovery. We have seen this in our discussion of Steps Ten, Eleven, and Twelve, which all suggest specific actions that will allow us to maintain our recovery on a daily basis.

At this point in our recovery, as we did earlier, we may want to examine some of the differences and similarities between smartphone addiction and some other addictions.

Abstinence

As discussed earlier, many traditional twelve-step programs suggest entire abstinence from the addictive substance or behavior. In Alcoholics Anonymous or Narcotics Anonymous, for instance, the recovering individual is expected to avoid using drugs or alcohol completely. If a person drinks one beer or takes one pill, it is considered a relapse.

AA and NA also operate using the concept of a "sobriety date" or a "clean date," which is the first day of complete and continuous abstinence from any use of alcohol or drugs. NA considers alcohol to be just another drug, and in AA, a person abusing drugs other than alcohol is not considered sober.

This suggestion of complete abstinence regarding alcohol and drugs is understandable in twelve-step programs where the addiction is to these substances. For an alcoholic getting drunk just once can lead to a fatal DUI, and someone who uses heroin or cocaine just once can die immediately.

We also earlier discussed the phenomenon of craving that occurs in an addict. Because of this, chances are great that the alcoholic or addict who drinks or uses will lose control again and in short order be back into a hopeless state. It should be clear that complete abstinence is reasonable and perhaps essential in programs like NA or AA. But such an absolute approach to abstinence is unreasonable in most cases for smartphone addiction.

How then shall we define abstinence in our twelve-step program for smartphone addiction? We will also need to define the concept of a recovery date and relate it to our conception of abstinence.

We determined earlier that while smartphone addiction is

a real addiction with potentially tragic consequences, the use of smartphone technology is difficult to avoid in contemporary society. One might even say that it is becoming effectively impossible to live in our society without some form of connected computing technology. Therefore, complete abstinence from use of a smartphone is an unrealistic goal for most of us.

To find a twelve-step program that offers some ideas for us, we can look at other traditional programs.

Complete abstinence from food is clearly an unachievable goal for members of Overeaters Anonymous. OA obviously does not suggest their members do not eat at all; however, the concept of abstinence is still utilized in the OA program.

This offers us a start towards our own definition. For our purposes we are looking at avoiding the obsessive and uncontrolled use of our smartphone technology. Especially, we will want to avoid using smartphone technology in a manner that causes harm to others. If we have worked through the twelve steps for smartphone addiction to the best of our ability, we should be able to recognize obsessive and uncontrolled use and thus utilize the technology in a controlled and thoughtful manner.

This is essentially the argument for abstinence in smartphone addiction. The idea is that we know in our heart after working the twelve steps and continuing to live the program, whether we are being abstinent on a regular basis or not.

For Smartphone Addiction we will define abstinence as follows, "Abstinence for smartphone addiction is the action of refraining from compulsive and selfish behaviors related to our smartphone use and using the technology in a controlled and unselfish manner by living the Twelve Steps for Smartphone Addiction as a way of life."

Clean Date

What about the concept of a clean date? That is, some date from which to measure our progress in continuous recovery from smartphone addiction.

As noted above, in AA and NA members track their recovery using the day of complete abstinence from any alcohol or drugs. Thus, a person might say, "I've got 30 days clean." Or one may declare something like this, "I will have one year sober next month if I don't drink before then."

However, if they drink or use the sobriety counter restarts. In twelve-step meetings, it is common to hear utterances like "I had sixty five days but I drank last week so now I am back in the program and I have five days sober."

The sobriety or clean date is thus very clearly defined.

How then shall we define a clean date for our program of recovery from smartphone addiction? Perhaps only time will tell. As more people use this twelve-step approach for smartphone addiction a useful and practical definition may be developed. Also, as meetings form there will naturally develop a growing fellowship of recovering smartphone addicts interacting. From this experience a proper perspective on the issue of a clean date may arise.

But for now let us say that the clean date for a person recovering from smartphone addiction is the date the decision is made to try to achieve abstinence on a daily basis from uncontrolled and obsessive use.

This means that the concept of relapse must be viewed differently, especially as it relates to the concept of a clean date. Many people will question whether on a given occasion they used their device in an uncontrolled manner, and since we use these devices all the time, it may be difficult to ascertain.

Nevertheless, most of the time in our hearts we will know if we have engaged in the selfish and uncontrolled use of our smartphone. Our goal then will be to use Steps Ten, Eleven, and Twelve to examine our behavior and motives, and resolve to do better tomorrow. If we are living our program of recovery as a way of life and trying consistently to examine our smartphone use with the principles of our program as our guide, we will have maintained our abstinence.

Since it is so closely related to the concept of a clean date, relapse as a concept also may become better defined and interpreted as experience grows with the use of the steps and the fellowship.

Service Work

In traditional twelve-step programs, service work is considered of paramount importance in maintaining abstinence over time. In our discussion on Step Twelve, we learned that trying to help others with the same affliction is one of the more crucial elements of any twelve-step program. This is a particular, and particularly important, form of service work.

Yet the concept of service work in recovery is much broader in scope. While trying to carry the message of our program of recovery to others is crucial, it is important to be of service in other areas as well. This is strongly emphasized in traditional twelve-step programs.

As previously covered, the basic and simple idea is that it is harder to think about ourselves and thus harder to be selfish and self-centered while we are doing something to try to help someone else. This includes any kind of service we might perform, with the important caveat that our primary intention is not some overt reward or benefit for ourselves.

It is also important to understand that we need not feel especially passionate or enthusiastic about the service work we have chosen to participate in. Especially if we are asked to do something. One of the ways we change our lives and ourselves is by changing our actions, and thereby our thinking and motives.

Wait, you might say. Is it not backward? Do we not change our thinking and motives, and then our behavior?

That may seem logical, but one of the primary mechanisms by which twelve-step programs work is through specific suggested actions. In fact, one alternate and well-accepted perspective is to say that a twelve-step program of recovery *is* a simple set of suggested spiritual actions.

A very common aphorism heard in twelve-step circles is "You can act your way into right thinking, but you can't think your way into right actions." The idea is that since we have been selfish and self-centered for so long our thinking is skewed towards these same qualities. Our minds, at least initially, are not to be trusted because a misty haze of self-centered thoughts clouds our motives.

However, it is also true that we have worked through all twelve steps of recovery by now. Thus, we have had the promised spiritual awakening and consequently our thoughts and motives have changed. We have a good understanding of our past selfish motives and subsequent bad behaviors. We see how these actions have harmed others and ourselves. We realize that with the help of our higher power and our fellows that we can recognize and thus avoid acting on our defects of character.

However, it is also true that experience shows that our thoughts and motives have a tendency to regress quickly back into selfishness. This is one of the primary mechanisms of relapse. A person starts to think too much about them self, dwells in self-pity, fear, and anger, and relapses back into the addictive behavior.

In traditional twelve-step programs then, there is an especially strong value placed on service work. Experience shows that doing good things for other people, whether they are addicts or not, is one the most important things we can do to maintain our recovery. We will thus follow the lead of other programs and suggest service work as a crucial element in our program of recovery for smartphone addiction.

We might broadly delineate service work into two primary categories, service work within our program of recovery and service work outside our program.

Service Work in Our Program

We have emphasized the importance of trying to carry the message of recovery to other smartphone addicts. It is one of the components of Step Twelve, and one of the key factors differentiating the twelve-step approach from other forms of addiction treatment. The message we are trying to carry is that an effective program of recovery for addiction to smartphone technology exists and that it has worked for us.

However, in traditional twelve-step programs, there are other forms of service as well. One form of service in a twelve-step program has to with the operation of a twelve-step meeting. These roles assumed by individuals to perform a certain service function for a particular meeting are called commitments. Thus, a person may have a commitment to make coffee for the meeting, or a commitment to creating a phone list for the meeting. The twelve-step meetings cannot function without people who are committed to fulfilling their service role.

Twelve-step programs usually have volunteers who go into rehab programs, jails, and other institutions to carry the message of recovery to other addicts. These are a type of service commitment as well.

Another form of service in twelve-step programs is to fill roles in the larger twelve-step organization structure. As AA and other twelve-step organizations like it grew, they found a need for a larger hierarchical service structure. Individuals are named to fill those roles.

For our program of recovery from smartphone addiction, these additional types of service roles will become clearly defined as experience with the program and meetings develops over time. Service to meetings will naturally occur first, with service in a larger structure coming later as necessary.

Service Work Outside Our Program

As mentioned above, while service within the program, especially carrying the message to others with our addiction, is of primary importance, experience shows that virtually any type of selfless service is important for us as well.

Moreover, service to others can be a crucial factor in maintaining abstinence from compulsive use behaviors.

The idea is again the simple and effective one that we are not thinking of ourselves when we are doing something for someone else. There is also the intuitive knowledge we all have that we feel better about ourselves after doing something good for someone else. Thus, while getting out of self is a benefit, another is the sometimes-subtle but lasting afterglow that occurs when we have performed some type of service work.

For our program of recovery from smartphone addiction, in particular, this service to others is initially of paramount importance. For one, there are as of yet no meetings and no service structure. Thus, while we may carry the message to other smartphone addicts, there are now currently few opportunities for other types of service within the program.

Still, outside our program of recovery for smartphone addiction service opportunities abound. We can volunteer at a homeless shelter and help those less fortunate than we. Lonely senior citizens who have led amazing lives often need companions. There are many gifted yet underprivileged children in need of mentors or tutors. The tragedy of unwanted animals offers a potential chance for us to save a life.

All of these service work opportunities present an opportunity for us to stop thinking about ourselves and refrain from engaging in selfish behaviors related to the use of smartphone technology.

Service work also brings us closer to our higher power. Regardless of our specific religious beliefs, we should all agree by this point in our spiritual journey that part of the reason we are here on earth is to help others. We have a special gift in being able to touch the lives of fellow addicts, but we can also do much more for others as well. Our connection with our higher power strengthens as we engage in these selfless efforts with no expectation of reward, as we can be certain that as least one component of "Our higher power's will for us" is service work for others.

SMARTPHONE ADDICTS ANONYMOUS FELLOWSHIP AND STATEMENT OF PURPOSE

The publication of the Twelve Steps for Smartphone Addiction also calls for the creation of a new fellowship patterned after Alcoholics Anonymous and other traditional twelve-step programs.

The primary purpose of Smartphone Addicts Anonymous is to provide a spiritual solution based on the twelve steps for the challenge of addiction to smartphones and to carry the message of recovery contained in the steps to others with the same challenge.

Smartphone Addicts Anonymous Meetings

As most people are aware, twelve-step meetings are one of the most important elements of traditional twelve-step programs. A special magic occurs in a twelve-step meeting.

From a clinical perspective, the effectiveness of group therapy is evidence-based and widely accepted. Especially when the members of the group share a common affliction, whether the meeting is twelve-step based or not. For instance, there are grief-counseling groups where all the members share a common issue, but they are not necessarily a twelve-step program. As a society, we may take the effectiveness and ubiquity of group therapy for granted now.

However, this was not always the case. In fact, this focus on a shared addiction is one of the key differentiating factors that Alcoholics Anonymous developed, and which other twelve-step based programs have built upon. That is, a "singleness of purpose" for the group, by which the group focuses primarily, and in theory only, on the specific addiction.

Historically, as we have seen earlier, AA grew out of the Oxford Group. The Oxford Group eventually disbanded at least in part because it tried to be all things to all people. It tried to help alcoholics, but also thieves, adulterers, and essentially anyone who wanted to apply Christian principles to their problems of living. This is not a judgment on the motives of the group but only on the fact that without a singleness of purpose it proved to be less effective than AA for the issue of alcoholism specifically.

The founders of AA eventually recognized this and started their own meetings, with a primary focus on alcoholism. Now we have twelve-step groups and other types of meetings for almost any malady known to humankind, and this is another of the wonderful, unexpected, and beautiful outcomes of Alcoholics Anonymous.

Thus, the call for the creation of the fellowship of Smartphone Addicts Anonymous and meetings based on AA meetings and those of other traditional twelve-step programs.

Meetings of Smartphone Addicts Anonymous will be of great effectiveness in helping members to maintain abstinence. For one thing, the meetings might be structured such that smartphones are not allowed to be used during a meeting. Thus, at least for one hour, or whatever is the duration of the meeting, an individual must control their smartphone use. These meetings also offer opportunities to help other smartphone addicts.

Most importantly though, twelve-step meetings will provide a place for those with a smartphone addiction to go to find an opportunity for recovery. Such meetings are also extremely helpful for those already in recovery, allowing them to reinforce the nature of their addiction and the power of the solution provided through the twelve steps.

With a fellowship and meetings of Smartphone Addicts Anonymous in place, the use of the Twelve Steps for Smartphone Addiction will grow, and provide an effective spiritual solution for this important and dangerous contemporary affliction.

CONCLUSION

Smartphone technology has assumed a dominant role in the lives of a large percentage of the human beings on this planet and has achieved that position with unnerving speed and power.

Many aspects of our lives are controlled by smartphone technology, with more coming online each day, weaving an interconnected network of information, which assumes so much power in our lives that we may feel completely out of control in the face of its overwhelming ubiquity.

This web of smartphone technology ensnares us, intelligently designed to reward us for progressively increasing usage. The phenomenon of craving produced through this cleverly architected and extraordinarily complex system is satiated only through more use and eventually leaves us powerless over its siren call.

As we attempt to come to terms with this unprecedented global explosion of smartphone usage, one implication of which is a certain percentage of real smartphone addicts, we as a society will hopefully realize the importance of applying the twelve steps to this new addiction.

In this work we have reviewed all twelve steps and applied them to smartphone addiction. We have seen that the twelve steps can provide a spiritual way of life that can solve our addiction to smartphones on a daily basis.

How then shall we summarize the ultimate meaning of the twelve steps?

During the last years of his life, Dr. Bob Smith, one of the two co-founders of AA, developed colon cancer. Dr. Bob has been called the "Prince of the twelve steppers" in AA because of the thousands of men and women he helped get sober. By all accounts he was an amazingly charitable human being and gave selflessly to others from the time he got sober until his untimely demise.

AA held its first International Convention in 1950, the year of Dr. Bob's death. By this time the Fellowship of Alcoholics Anonymous had grown exponentially into a worldwide phenomenon from its humble beginnings in 1935.

In what turned out to be his last talk, Dr. Bob, his body wracked with cancer, made it up to the podium in front of the 20,000 attendees at the St. Louis Convention Center. Here he delivered a revered speech of only three and a half minutes, that is renowned for its power and simplicity.

For our present purposes, the most important portion of the talk is contained in the following sentences.

"Our twelve steps, when simmered down to the last, resolve themselves into the words love and service. We understand what love is and we understand what service is. So let's bear those two things in mind."

This author has not encountered a more succinct, elegant, and correct summarization of the meaning of the twelve steps. Now that we have realized a spiritual awakening through working all twelve steps to the best of our ability, we should be able to see how true these words are.

The twelve steps have proven so successful in providing a solution to many addictions in large part because they are based on timeless and correct spiritual principles. The twelve steps can provide a spiritual solution to smartphone addiction based on these same timeless principles, which resolve themselves simply and beautifully into love and service.

Made in the USA
Middletown, DE
27 February 2022

61880704R00096